Business
PLUS

Preparing for the workplace

Margaret Helliwell

CAMBRIDGE
UNIVERSITY PRESS

Teacher's Manual 1

CAMBRIDGE
UNIVERSITY PRESS

University Printing House, Cambridge CB2 8BS, United Kingdom

One Liberty Plaza, 20th Floor, New York, NY 10006, USA

477 Williamstown Road, Port Melbourne, VIC 3207, Australia

314–321, 3rd Floor, Plot 3, Splendor Forum, Jasola District Centre, New Delhi – 110025, India

79 Anson Road, #06–04/06, Singapore 079906

Cambridge University Press is part of the University of Cambridge.

It furthers the University's mission by disseminating knowledge in the pursuit of education, learning and research at the highest international levels of excellence.

www.cambridge.org
Information on this title: www.cambridge.org/9781107668805

First published 2014
Reprinted 2019

Printed in Italy by Rotolito S.p.A.

ISBN 978-1-107-66880-5 paperback Teacher's Manual 1
ISBN 978-1-107-64068-9 paperback Student's Book 1

Additional resources for this publication at www.cambridge.org/businessplus

Contents

Plan of the Student's Book   iv

Introduction   viii

Unit 1   **Nice to meet you**   2

Unit 2   **In the office**   7

Unit 3   **On the phone**   14

Unit 4   **Buying and selling**   19

Unit 5   **What are you doing tomorrow?**   25

Unit 6   **Out and about**   31

Unit 7   **Tell me about your company**   37

Unit 8   **Let's eat out**   43

Unit 9   **Work and play**   49

Unit 10   **Come again soon!**   53

Plan of the Student's Book

	Business situation	Grammar focus	Listening and speaking	Vocabulary focus
Before you begin Page viii				
Unit 1 **Nice to meet you** Pages 1–8	At the airport	1 *To be* 2 Present simple	Opening and closing conversations	1 Numbers 2 Countries and regions
Unit 2 **In the office** Pages 9–16	Types of office	1 *There is . . . , there are . . .* 2 Adverbs of frequency	A typical day Talking about a day in the life of a famous person	1 Office equipment 2 Words that go together (1)
TOEIC® practice Pages 17–18				
Unit 3 **On the phone** Pages 19–26	Can I take a message?	Present simple and present continuous	On the phone Talking about cell phones	1 Spelling names and saying numbers 2 Telephone language
Unit 4 **Buying and selling** Pages 27–34	Helping customers	1 *some* and *any* 2 *much* and *many*	Shopping habits Talking about shopping: good and bad service	1 Giving directions 2 Words that go together (2)
TOEIC® practice Pages 35–36				
Unit 5 **What are you doing tomorrow?** Pages 37–44	Making an appointment	Present continuous for future plans	Making plans and suggestions	1 Days, months, dates 2 Telling the time

Reading	Culture focus	Business writing	Learning outcomes
			Students can . . .
Talking about jobs	Meeting and greeting		<ul><li>welcome a visitor.</li><li>ask for and give personal information.</li><li>open, continue, and close a conversation.</li><li>ask for and tell people numbers.</li><li>talk about countries and regions.</li><li>understand a text about different jobs.</li><li>talk about greeting people in different countries.</li></ul>
Offices around the world		Emails	<ul><li>talk about different types of office.</li><li>describe an office and talk about routines.</li><li>ask about and describe a typical day.</li><li>talk about office equipment and where it is.</li><li>understand a text about different offices.</li><li>write an email to ask for information.</li></ul>
The unbreakable cell phone	Business cards in Asia		<ul><li>understand telephone phrases.</li><li>talk about what people are doing now.</li><li>understand telephone messages and talk about cell phones.</li><li>spell names.</li><li>use telephone language.</li><li>understand a text about new smartphones.</li><li>read a text about business cards in Asia.</li></ul>
Showrooming		An inquiry	<ul><li>understand conversations in a store.</li><li>use *some/any* and *much/many*.</li><li>talk about shopping habits and service in stores.</li><li>understand and give directions.</li><li>use words that go together.</li><li>understand a text about the future of shopping.</li><li>write an email asking for product information.</li></ul>
London to Beijing in two days	Communication styles		<ul><li>understand a conversation about making appointments.</li><li>discuss future plans.</li><li>understand a discussion about plans and make suggestions.</li><li>talk about times and dates.</li><li>understand the main idea of a text about future plans.</li><li>understand different communication styles.</li></ul>

Plan of the Student's Book

	Business situation	Grammar focus	Listening and speaking	Vocabulary focus
Unit 6 **Out and about** *Pages 45–52*	Customer service in a hotel	Comparing people, places, and things	Giving advice Talking about traveling	1 Traveling 2 Describing pictures
TOEIC® practice *Pages 53–54*				
Unit 7 **Tell me about your company** *Pages 55–62*	The story of a company	1 Past simple – regular verbs 2 Past simple – irregular verbs	Successful Asian companies Talking about successful companies	1 Countries and nationalities 2 *Make* and *do*
Unit 8 **Let's eat out** *Pages 63–70*	Entertaining in the business world	1 Modal verbs 2 Countable and uncountable nouns	In a food court	1 Food and drink 2 Invitations
TOEIC® practice *Pages 71–72*				
Unit 9 **Work and play** *Pages 73–80*	During and after work	1 *-ing* or *to*-infinitive 2 Connecting words	Travel and leisure in Asia	1 *play/do/go . . .* 2 Describing leisure activities
Unit 10 **Come again soon!** *Pages 81–88*	Saying goodbye	1 The *will*-future 2 Grammar quiz	The workplace in 2025	1 Saying hello and goodbye 2 Vocabulary quiz
TOEIC® practice *Pages 89–90*				

Partner files *Pages 91–94*   **Irregular verbs** *Page 95*   **Transcripts** *Pages 96–111*

Reading	Culture focus	Business writing	Learning outcomes
			Students can . . .
The Richmond Hotel, Jakarta		A confirmation	<ul><li>change a hotel reservation on the phone.</li><li>compare people, places, and things.</li><li>talk about vacations and ways to travel.</li><li>use different words to talk about traveling.</li><li>describe pictures.</li><li>understand comments on a hotel.</li><li>write a confirmation email.</li></ul>
Top jobs for women	Conversation taboos		<ul><li>understand somebody talking about a company.</li><li>talk about things in the past.</li><li>research and present information about a company.</li><li>talk about countries and nationalities.</li><li>ask and answer questions with *make* and *do*.</li><li>understand a text about women in top jobs.</li><li>understand conversation taboos.</li></ul>
Special requests on MJets		Invitations	<ul><li>understand an invitation and a conversation in a restaurant.</li><li>use the modal verbs *can*, *must*, *have to*, *need to*.</li><li>use countable and uncountable nouns.</li><li>talk about a restaurant menu.</li><li>talk about food, drinks, and a favorite dish.</li><li>invite somebody and say yes or no to an invitation.</li><li>understand a text about a private jet service.</li><li>invite somebody and write yes or no to an invitation.</li></ul>
Tourists in Thailand	Body language in Asia		<ul><li>understand a conversation about work and leisure.</li><li>use *-ing* and *to*-infinitive forms after some verbs.</li><li>use connecting words.</li><li>understand and talk about travel and leisure in Asia.</li><li>talk about leisure time activities.</li><li>understand a text about tourism in Thailand.</li><li>understand body language in Asian countries.</li></ul>
The ASEAN Economic Community		A thank-you email	<ul><li>understand people saying goodbye.</li><li>use *will* and *won't* to talk about the future.</li><li>listen to and talk about life in the future.</li><li>say hello and goodbye and use prepositions after verbs.</li><li>understand an article about the advantages of the ASEAN Economic Community.</li><li>write a thank-you email.</li></ul>

Introduction

Welcome to **Business Plus 1**. This Teacher's Manual contains a step-by-step guide to teaching each section of the Student's Book, as well as useful tips, keys to the exercises, and model answers to speaking and writing tasks.

The emphasis of the **Business Plus** course is on speaking, listening, reading, and writing English within business contexts. In each unit learners are guided through a variety of student-centered activities aimed at building their language skills and confidence. New grammar structures and vocabulary are introduced systematically and followed up with controlled practice activities. There are also freer practice activities that allow students to develop their fluency. State-of-the-art business topics keep students' motivation at a high level. All audio material for student's book listening activities, including the listening practice for the TOEIC® exam, can be downloaded from http://www.cambridge.org/businessplus. Every unit contains interesting and attractive pictures and cartoons that can be used to get students talking.

With further support available on the website, both teachers and students can enjoy a new teaching and learning experience with **Business Plus**.

What is *Business Plus*?

Business Plus is a three-level course in business communication skills, designed with a specifically Asian focus to meet the growing demand for workplace English in the region. **Business Plus** prepares students to communicate effectively in an English-speaking business environment, both in social and work-related situations. **Business Plus** provides input and practice in all four language skills, and develops students' cultural awareness in business situations.

Key features of *Business Plus*

+ **Business Plus** is aimed at pre-work-experience university students, but can equally be used with in-service learners.

+ Each level includes integrated TOEIC® practice pages to familiarize students with the test formats and help them improve their language skills specifically for the test. They serve at the same time to review and consolidate language practiced in the units.

+ An *I can*-statement at the end of each stage focuses on the learning outcome of the section.

+ *Key words* relevant to the topic can be found at the bottom of the pages in sections 1 to 3 of each unit. The key words are then tested in the *Vocabulary focus* section.

+ Many recordings highlight the importance of being able to communicate in English not only with native speakers but also with non-native speakers in Asia, through the use of speakers with authentic Asian accents.

+ Regular "Culture focus" pages aim to promote intercultural awareness.

+ Topics focus on business in Asia and between Asian nations, with particular emphasis on ASEAN countries.

Who is *Business Plus 1* for?

Business Plus 1 is designed for pre-work-experience adult students at the false beginner (A1/A2) level. The course aims to prepare students for English in the business world by activating and further developing the language the students have studied in the past. It provides a wide variety of communicative tasks and adequate opportunity for students to practice the skills of speaking, listening, reading, and writing in business situations.

How is *Business Plus 1* organized?

Business Plus 1 consists of 10 units. Each unit has six sections:

1 Business situation
2 Grammar focus
3 Listening and speaking
4 Vocabulary focus
5 Reading
6 Culture focus or Business writing.

In every second unit there are two pages of TOEIC® practice. *Partner files* can be found on pages 91–94 in the Student's Book and a list of irregular verbs for reference is on page 95.

Business situation

Each unit begins with a *Business situation*, which provides an introduction to the main topic and the key language of the unit. The *Business situation* usually involves listening to a conversation in which the key grammar structures and key vocabulary of the unit are used in a typical business context.

As international business communication frequently takes place between non-native speakers, the conversations are spoken not only by native speakers – mainly from North America and Australia – but also by a number of competent non-native speakers with a variety of authentic Asian accents.

Grammar focus

The *Grammar focus* provides analysis and practice of the key grammar structures introduced in the *Business situation*. It is assumed that students will have already had exposure to English grammar before taking this course; therefore, this section is designed to revise and expand on grammar previously learned. Using key examples from the *Business situation*, students are guided to discover the essential rules of form and use. This is followed by a wide range of both controlled practice activities – including completion, multiple choice, and matching exercises – and free, communicative activities in pairs or groups.

Listening and speaking

As in the *Business situations*, the recordings in this section include both native speakers and non-native speakers with Asian accents. A wide variety of listening activities includes comprehension questions, completion, sentence completion, matching, correcting mistakes or false statements, true-false exercises, and completing charts. The aim of all tasks is to help students develop their listening skills.

The speaking activities in this section include guided discussions about the topic of the unit. Prompts give students confidence and help them formulate their answers. There are further student-centered communication activities in other sections of the book, including partner interviews, information-transfer tasks, guided conversations, and *Now you* tasks, where students talk about themselves. A wide range of pair work and group work activities mean that even in larger classes students are given ample opportunity to speak. Additional notes for the teacher concerning the organization of speaking activities can be found in the relevant sections of this manual.

Vocabulary focus

This section is designed to enhance students' vocabulary with particular reference to the topic of the unit. Emphasis has been placed on core vocabulary in the business world, and throughout the course there are opportunities for students to use this vocabulary in various contexts. Students focus on patterns such as word collocations, word families, word formation, antonyms, synonyms, and prepositions. They are also given opportunities to learn and practice useful phrases for making conversation; telephoning; giving directions; describing pictures; making, accepting, and declining invitations; and making suggestions.

As mentioned above, sections 1 to 3 feature key words that are tested at the end of the *Vocabulary focus* section.

Reading

The reading texts in each unit of the **Business Plus** series are part of *Asian Business Online*, an online magazine that features stimulating articles about topics particularly relevant to Asian learners. As students move through the course, the reading texts become longer and more challenging, and students are exposed to increasing amounts of new vocabulary.

Tasks are aimed at helping students to develop good reading skills, such as looking for the main ideas, skimming for general understanding, and scanning for detail. The reading texts can also be used to extend vocabulary and to practice pronunciation.

Culture focus

In every second unit there is a *Culture focus* where special attention is paid to the importance of cultural awareness in business situations. Students look at their own cultures and learn about those of other countries. Topics include meeting and greeting, communication styles, conversation taboos, and body language. The aim of the *Culture focus* is to heighten students' awareness of the potential misunderstandings that can arise when doing business with people from other countries.

Business writing

This section aims to help students achieve fluency in business writing. The business writing tasks in the **Business Plus** series range from business emails to the agenda and minutes of a meeting. Models are provided for students to analyze and imitate.

TOEIC® practice

This comes after every two units. Practice for the TOEIC® Speaking and Writing test, as well as for the Listening and Reading test, is based on real test formats, but at the same time vocabulary, structures, and topics from the preceding course units are revised and consolidated. A wide variety of TOEIC® exam formats are covered. Details of the formats and the strategies students need in order to master exam tasks are provided in the relevant sections of the Teacher's Manual.

Partner files

Throughout the course there are opportunities for students to engage in communicative pair work. At the back of the Student's Book, seven *Partner files* provide information and language prompts for one of the partners.

Irregular verbs

A list of irregular verbs is included at the back of the Student's Book for reference.

Scripts

The listening scripts are helpful when focusing students' attention on examples of the key grammar structures or vocabulary used in the unit, to check the answers to a listening activity, or for students to read aloud after a listening activity for pronunciation practice and consolidation.

Useful tips

Below are some useful tips that can be referred to throughout the course.

TIP 1: Seven-step listening

The following procedure can be used for many of the listening activities in the book:

Step 1: Before listening, set the scene. This gives the listening task a context and makes it easier for students to understand. There are various ways of setting the scene, and suggestions are made in each unit.

Step 2: Make sure the instructions are clear. Read the instructions to the class or have students read them aloud. Ask them to read any statements, questions, charts, etc. carefully, either silently or aloud. Check comprehension.

Step 3: Play the recording once or twice as needed. Students do the tasks.

Step 4: Students compare their answers in pairs or groups.

Step 5: Go over the answers with the class.

Step 6: Play the recording again. Students follow the script.

Step 7: Students work in pairs or groups. Each takes a role, and they read aloud the conversation in the script. Monitor the groups or pairs, correcting pronunciation and intonation. It is not necessary to wait for the end of the activity to give feedback as the main focus here is on form and not communication.

TIP 2: Teaching reading comprehension

One important consideration for a teacher is: Am I teaching my students to read or am I testing their reading comprehension? The tasks in the *Reading* section of **Business Plus** are intended as a means of helping learners to improve their reading ability; therefore, students must be carefully guided to read in different ways and at different speeds. In the *Reading* section they can learn to:

skim a text – i.e., read for a quick, general understanding, ignoring unknown words;

scan a text – i.e., run through the text on the look-out for relevant details. When those details are spotted, the reader may then

read intensively – i.e., for full comprehension. This may involve looking up words in a dictionary.

Before every reading activity, it is important to make it clear to students why they are reading, what they are looking for, and which technique they should use.

These techniques can only be practiced as silent reading, as each student has to read at his or her own pace. But the teacher may want to finish the *Reading* section by having the text read aloud to practice pronunciation and intonation.

The texts in "Asian Business Online" recycle some of the previous vocabulary in the unit, but they also introduce new vocabulary, which may need to be pre-taught, depending on students' level and abilities.

TIP 3: Communicative pair work and group work

Organizing pairs and groups: With pair work there is always the problem of what happens when there is an odd number of students. One possible solution is that the teacher works with a student, but this means he or she is not available to monitor the activity in the class. A better solution is if three students work together, two form a team and take turns to talk to the third one. The group of three should, of course, be changed frequently. Likewise, partners should be changed for partner activities to ensure that everyone has the opportunity to work with and get to know as many other students as possible. It is important that the teacher take the responsibility for assigning pairs, thus ensuring that students work with different partners, and weaker and stronger students can be put together.

A note on large classes

If you are teaching in large classes, the organization of pair work and group work can be difficult to facilitate. However, there are a number of things that can be done to make this easier:

1   Pair work doesn't have to be sitting down! To add some variety, ask students to do a task standing up or walking around the classroom.

2   For group work, ask a pair of students to turn around and work with the pair behind / in front of them.

3   Ask one or two pairs of (stronger) students to model an activity first, before the rest of the class begins. This increases the chances of learners understanding exactly what they are required to do.

4   Get students to repeat tasks with another partner sitting on the other side / behind / in front, or seated with their backs to each other.

Introducing an activity: In group work and pair work it is essential that students know exactly what they have to do before they begin. Clear instructions are given in the Student's Book for all activities, so it should be sufficient to read or have students read the instructions. However, if a little more help is necessary, the teacher can give a demonstration with one or more partners while other students watch.

Talking about . . .

This type of activity involves both pair and group work, as a cooperative learning environment can serve to build students' confidence and promote their willingness to speak. The *Talking about* . . . tasks involve several preparatory steps, and prompts are given for each step.

Example:

Step 1: Students think about their task and make notes – it may be a list of ideas or key words.

Step 2: Students work in pairs or groups and compare or pool their ideas.

Step 3: Students tell the class their ideas – one student can speak for the group or pair, or students can report individually.

Monitoring and following up an activity: In communicative group and pair work the teacher should monitor the pairs or groups, noting problems or mistakes. Error correction should not take place during communicative activities. The feedback phase comes after the activity. Write the error on the board – without indicating whose error it was – and ask the students to correct it. If necessary, further practice can be given. Now and then a group or pair of especially good students can be asked to repeat the activity while the rest of the class listens.

Nice to meet you

Unit aims

In Unit 1 students will
- practice meeting and introducing themselves and others.
- learn how to use *to be* and the present simple in statements, negatives, and questions.
- exchange personal information.
- develop skills for opening and closing conversations.
- understand and tell people numbers.
- talk about countries and regions.
- understand a text and write about jobs.
- learn and talk about greetings in different countries.

When you begin **Business Plus 1**, you are probably starting with a new group of students. The title of Unit 1 is *Nice to meet you*, and one important aim of the unit is that you and the students get to know each other. It will also give you an opportunity to assess the students' skills, even though they will have relatively little English at this stage.

Before you get started, it will be useful to introduce some classroom language such as:
Excuse me.
I don't know.
I don't understand.
Could you say it again, please?
What does . . . mean?
Could you speak more slowly, please?
You can introduce these expressions on the board or make a poster, leaving enough space to add more phrases later.
Ask: *What do you say if you want to ask a question? What do you say if someone speaks too fast?* etc. When you have elicited all the phrases on the board/poster, students write them down in their notebooks. The poster can stay in the classroom and have more phrases added later.

1 Business situation
At the airport

page 1

Before playing the recording, talk about the pictures. Ask students what they can see. In bigger classes you can ask students to work in pairs and describe the pictures to each other. Write the questions on the board:
What can you see in the pictures?
Where are the people?
Who are the people on the left?

Elicit: *We can see an Asian man and another man and a woman. The people are at the airport The people on the left are visitors.*
Tell students that the man on the right is Hiroshi Akimoto. The people on the left are Christine Klein and Robert Tomlin. They are Mr. Akimoto's visitors.

1A This task introduces useful phrases for meeting visitors. Follow Steps 2 to 5 of TIP 1 on page xi.

Answer key

1 Excuse me.
3 Yes, that's right.
5 Welcome to Osaka.
6 This is my colleague.
8 That's very kind.
9 How was your flight?
10 It was fine.

1B Follow Steps 2 to 5 of TIP 1 on page xi. As you go over the answers, you can ask students to correct the false statements.

Answer key

1 False	4 False
2 True	5 False
3 True	6 False

Finally, follow Steps 6 and 7 of TIP 1 on page xi, with students working in groups of three.

1C See TIP 3 on pages xii–xiii for guidelines to group work.

Groups should re-form and repeat the task with other members of the class, so that they get to know the names of several other students.

 ## 2 Grammar focus
The verb *to be* and the present simple
pages 2–3

2A Begin by providing a model for pronunciation. Focus students' attention on the four people. Ask students to repeat the questions and answers:

Say: *Where is Hiroshi Akimoto from? He's from Tokyo, Japan.*
Students repeat: *Where is Hiroshi Akimoto from? He's from Tokyo, Japan.*

Say: *Where is Lin Yao Chen from? She's from Taipei, Taiwan.*
Where is Christine Klein from? She's from Berlin, Germany.
Where is Robert Tomlin from? He's from Glasgow, Scotland.
Where is Hiroshi's company? It's in Osaka, Japan.
Where is Robert's company. It's in London, UK.
What is the name of Lin Yao's company? It's GameZ.
What is the name of Christine's company? It's Digital Design.
What's Hiroshi's job? He's a marketing manager.
What's Lin Yao's job? She's an IT data scientist.
What's Christine's job? She's a video game designer.
What's Robert's job? He's a product manager.

Draw students' attention to the tip on page 2. (*"He is a marketing manager. She is an IT data scientist."*) Further practice will be given in the *Reading* section.

Write the questions below on the board and ask students to work in pairs to ask and answer questions about the four people.
Where is . . . from?
Where is . . .'s company?
What's the name of . . .'s company?
What's . . .'s job?

Monitor the pairs.

2B Ask students to read the text. Give them the opportunity to ask about unknown vocabulary, although the main focus at this stage is on the verb *to be*. Students then work in pairs to complete the chart and compare their answers. In the feedback phase, put the chart on the board. Students can come up to the board and write in the correct forms. Students then do the second part of the task and underline the forms of *to be* in the text.

Answer key

The verb *to be*

Long form	Short form	Negative
he is	he's	*he isn't*
she is	she's	she isn't
they are	*they're*	they aren't

Hiroshi Akimoto and Lin Yao Chen **are** colleagues.
Hiroshi **is** a marketing manager.
Lin Yao **is** an IT data scientist.
Christine Klein and Robert Tomlin **are** colleagues, too.
But they **aren't** in the same department.
Christine **is** a video game designer.
Robert **is** a product manager.
She **isn't** English.
She**'s** German.

2C Students can work individually or in pairs to fill in the gaps with information from the text on page 2. Draw attention to the *-s* in the third person and two ways of pronouncing it:
works /wɜːks/   *likes* /laɪks/
comes /kʌmz/   *does* /dʌz/

Many students have problems with *do/does* in negatives and questions, so these forms will need highlighting.

Answer key

Present simple

Statements
Hiroshi **works** for GameZ. He **likes** his job.
Lin Yao **works** for GameZ, too. She also **likes** her job.

Hiroshi and Lin Yao **work** for GameZ.
They **like** their jobs.

Negatives
Christine comes from Berlin, but she **doesn't live** there.

Robert comes from Scotland, but he **doesn't live** there.

Christine and Robert **work** in London, but they **don't live** there.

Questions
A: Where **does** Lin Yao **work**?
B: She works in Osaka.
A: What **does** she **do**?
B: She's an IT data scientist.

A: Where **do** Hiroshi and Lin Yao **work**?
B: They work in Osaka.
A: What **do** they **do**?
B: He's a marketing manager. She's an IT data scientist.

Draw attention to the tip on page 3. If you wish to elaborate on this point, you could put students in groups or pairs to ask and answer questions about their family, friends, or neighbors.

Students ask: *What does your father do? What does your mother do? What does your neighbor do?*

2D Students work in pairs to complete the chart. In the feedback phase, put the chart on the board. Students can come up to the board and write in the correct forms.

Answer key

Present simple			
	Positive	**Negative**	**Questions**
I/you/ we/they	work	**don't work**	Do I/you/we/ they work?
he/she/ it	**works**	doesn't **work**	**Does he/she/ it work?**

2E See TIP 3 on page xii–xiii for guidelines to pair work. Pairs should re-form several times and repeat the task, thus giving students ample opportunity to get to know each other.

3 Listening and speaking
Opening and closing conversations
page 4

Before listening, ask students for their ideas on how to start a conversation. If necessary, refer them back to 1A.

3A Make sure the instructions are clear. Have students work individually or in pairs to do the task. Ask students to read out their answers. Do not correct, but ask for peer correction.
Then say: *Let us see if that is correct.* Play the recording once or twice as needed.

Answer key

1
A: Excuse me. Are you Ms. Lee?
B: Yes, that's right. You must be Mr. Tang.
A: Yes, I am. I'm sorry to keep you waiting.
B: That's all right.

2
A: Are you going to Indonesia on business?
B: Yes, I am. And you?
A: No, I'm going on vacation.
B: Lucky you!

3B Make sure the instructions are clear. Play the recording once or twice as needed. Go over the answers with the class, then move on to the question: *"What do you talk about in your country when you don't know somebody?"*

Answer key

food – language – vacations

3C Make sure the instructions are clear. Tell students you will play the recording three times. The first time they should just listen. The second time stop the recording after each sentence to give students time to write their answers. Play the recording a third time for students to check their answers. Discuss any problems and, if necessary, play parts of the recording again.

Answer key

1
A: Well, it was **nice to talk** to you.
B: Yes, I hope **we can meet again** sometime.
A: That would be great. I'll call you next time **I'm in town.**
B: Fine.

2
A: Would you **excuse me**? I have to go soon.
B: What time **does your plane** leave?
A: At six. So I really **have to hurry**.
B: **No problem**. Shall I call you a taxi?

3D Students work in pairs and read the conversations. Monitor the pairs, correcting pronunciation and intonation on the spot.

4 Vocabulary focus
Focus 1: Numbers
page 5

4A Before listening ask students what they can see in the picture and what they think they will hear. Follow Steps 2 to 6 of TIP 1 on page xi. The recording should be played at least twice.

Answer key

	Flight number	Destination	Gate
1	MH 537	*Bangkok*	E15
2	SQ 261	Singapore	A39
3	UA 9679	Chicago	B30
4	NH 489	Jakarta	D5
5	LH 3379	London	G8
6	TK 1789	Istanbul	C12

4B Before listening, tell students they are going to hear some telephone conversations. In each case the person who calls can't speak to the person he wanted, so somebody takes a message. Follow Steps 2 to 7 of TIP 1 on page xi, with students working in pairs.

Answer key

1 06 6347 7111
2 0044 871 527 864
3 02 2712 6543.
4 0062 2993 8876

4C Make sure the instructions are clear. Monitor the pairs and correct any errors in pronunciation and intonation on the spot.

4 Vocabulary focus
Focus 2: Countries and regions

> page 6

4D Before listening, set the scene. Ask students to look at the map and the countries that are named there. Do they know any other countries? Then follow Steps 2 to 6 of TIP 1 on page xi.

Answer key

My mother was born in **France**, my father in **Spain**, and they met on vacation in **Mexico**. I was born in **Great Britain**, but we also lived in the **United States** and **Canada** because my father worked there. I love traveling, especially to **Asia**. I have been to **Japan**, **Thailand**, and **South Korea**. I would like to go to **China**, too. But my next vacation will be in **South America**, **Brazil** and **Peru**. The only place that doesn't interest me much is **Antarctica**. I think it would be too cold!

4E Ask the class what they know about ASEAN and provide any missing information.

Background information
ASEAN stands for the Association of Southeast Asian Nations. It is a political and economic organization of ten countries: Brunei, Cambodia, Indonesia, Laos, Malaysia, Myanmar, the Philippines, Singapore, Thailand, and Vietnam. It has a population of about 600 million people.

Students do the task in pairs, then share their ideas with the class. The answer key gives only the countries named on the map on page 6. Students may have their own ideas.

Answer key

Countries in Asia: China, India, Indonesia, Japan, Malaysia, South Korea, Thailand

Countries in Europe: France, Germany, Great Britain, Italy, Russia, Spain

Countries in ASEAN: Indonesia, Malaysia, Thailand

Countries in Africa: Kenya, South Africa

Countries in South America: Brazil, Chile, Peru

Countries in North America: Canada, Mexico, the United States

4F The *Key words* task tests the key vocabulary that is at the bottom of pages 1–4. This can be done as homework.

Answer key

1 airport
2 colleague
3 department
4 designer
5 on vacation
6 topics – conversation
7 flight
8 Excuse me.

5 Reading
Talking about jobs

> page 7

Look at TIP 2 on page xii for general guidelines to reading tasks.

5A Have students work in pairs or groups to make their lists. In the feedback phase list the jobs on the board. You can use this list for an additional exercise after the reading task.

Have students skim the article to find any jobs from their list. This is the first time students have been asked to "skim the article", so you should explain to them what they have to do. Look at the guidelines on reading in TIP 2 on page xii. Skimming usually involves reading quickly, so set a time limit. Go over the answers with the class.

5B If you feel your students will be unable to cope with the text, you can pre-teach some vocabulary, e.g., *computer network*, *bookstore*, *customer*, *staff*. Have students read the text silently at first, and in pairs do the *Scanning for detail* task. Go over the answers with the class.

To provide additional practice for the tip on page 2 ("*He is a marketing manager. / She is an IT data scientist.*"), job vocabulary, and the verb *to be*, while students are reading, write some of the jobs which are on the board (see 5A) on pieces of paper. Give all or some students (depending on the size of the class) a "job," i.e., a piece of paper. In larger classes students can work in groups where two or three students per group have a "job." Then play "10 questions." Students can ask ten questions with *Are you a(n) . . . ? Do you . . . ?* The student with a job replies *Yes, I am, No, I'm not,* or *Yes, I do, No, I don't . . . .*

With better students the list of jobs can also be used for further practice of the third-person present simple.
Ask: *Where does a teacher work?*
Student: *He/She works in a school?*

5C This writing task can be given as homework or done in class. In any case, it should be handed in for individual correction. In the next lesson, you can deal with any general problems and give remedial work to the class or individuals.

6A Make sure the instructions are clear. Students can work individually or in pairs. Go over the answers with the class.

6B This task presents an opportunity to discuss cultural differences related to greetings. Question 1 focuses on informal situations and question 2 on formal situations. Ask students to describe the differences in each situation. Explain that in many Western cultures handshakes are important. This will lead you into task 6C.

6C Make sure the instructions are clear. Students can do this task individually or in pairs. Go over the answers with the class.

In the office

Unit aims

In Unit 2 students will
- talk about different types of offices.
- learn to use *there is* and *there are*.
- describe an office and office equipment.
- learn to use adverbs of frequency.
- ask and talk about daily routines.
- practice using the prepositions *in*, *on*, *under*.
- learn and use word collocations.
- read about offices around the world.
- write an email to ask for information.
- practice listening, speaking, reading, and writing for the TOEIC® test.

Before beginning a new unit, you might like to review the previous unit. Ask your students what they learned, what they enjoyed, what they didn't enjoy and why. The answers will give you some insight into how students feel about the course and their own progress, and help you make adjustments at an early stage.

In Unit 2 we look at offices and office equipment. There is quite a lot of new vocabulary in this unit, so now is the time to find out if your students are keeping a vocabulary notebook. How do they organize their notebooks? It may be helpful to show students that there are more effective ways of organizing vocabulary than alphabetical lists. People often remember words in groups that have something in common. Although the way we group our words is personal, you can make the following suggestions with examples from Unit 1:
- words with the same initial consonant: *colleague, company, conversation, customer*
- word fields: JOBS: *marketing manager, IT data scientist, video game designer, product manager, computer specialist, department manager, hotel receptionist*
- word families: *to design, design, designer*

1 Business situation
Types of office

page 9

1A Discuss the pictures with your students. You can also ask, *What other things can you see in the two offices?* (*cell phone, computer, coffee cup, plant,* etc.), thus giving students the opportunity to use words they already know.

Answer key

B	a lot of people
A	a man alone
B	family photos
B	four desks
A	a man without a jacket
B	a man with a jacket
A	an orange office chair
A/B	telephones

1B Before listening, ask students: *What are the good things and the bad things about a one-person office? What are the good things and the bad things about an open-plan office?*

You may want to pre-teach the key words at the bottom of page 9 as they will help students understand the recording.

Follow Steps 2 to 6 of TIP 1 on page xi, although you might prefer not to let students see the script until they have completed 2A. Finally, you can have students read the script aloud. Correct pronunciation and intonation on the spot.

Answer key

		Robert	Lin Yao
2	There are 10 colleagues.		✔
3	There's no-one to talk to.		✔
4	Colleagues want to chat.	✔	
5	There's always a lot of noise.	✔	
6	It's a bit noisy and hectic.		✔

1C This task reinforces some of the vocabulary from 1B. Students can complete the sentences individually, then compare their answers with a partner. Go over the answers with the class.

Answer key

2 communicate
3 desk
4 waste
5 noise
6 noisy
7 freedom

2 Grammar focus
Focus 1: *There is . . . , there are . . .*
page 10

2A Play the recording again. Have students fill in the missing words and compare their answers with a partner. Go over the answers with the class.

Answer key

1 **There's** a desk, a chair, and a file cabinet in Robert's office.
2 **There's** always a lot of noise in an open-plan office.
3 Lin Yao doesn't want a one-person office because **there's** no one to talk to.
4 **There are** 10 colleagues in Lin Yao's office.
5 In a one-person office, **there are** only four walls to look at.

2B Elicit the rule. Students often confuse *There's a . . .* and *It's a . . . .* The difference is that *it* defines something that has a name. In the sentences:
The office is small. ***It's*** *a one-person office.*
There's *a computer on the table.*
it refers to the office; *there* doesn't refer to anything specific.

Point out the short form *there's*, which is used in spoken English. The script uses the short form *there's*, but keeps the long form *there are*, as there could be difficulties with the pronunciation and understanding of *there're*. For further practice you could go back to the pictures of the offices on page 9 and talk about them again using *there is* and *there are*. Put the negative forms *there isn't* and *there aren't* on the board. Students will need these forms in 2C.

Rule

Use *there is* with a **singular** word.
Use *there are* with a **plural** word.

2C This task provides intensive practice of *there is* and *there are*. This is the first *Partner files* activity in the Student's Book, and it might be the first time your students have ever done such an information gap activity, so it is important to explain exactly how it functions. Stress that students must not show each other their information! Put students in pairs and ask Student A not to look at the information on this page, but to go straight to Partner file 1 on page 91. When you are certain that students have understood the instructions, start the activity. See TIP 3 on pages xii–xiii for further guidelines on pair work.

Answer key

	Student A	Student B
1	There's a glass of water on the desk.	There's a cup of tea on the desk.
2	There are four pens on the desk. (There are three pens on the desk and one on the notepad.)	There are two pens on the desk (and none on the notepad.)
3	There are four blue files on the desk.	There are five files on the desk. They are all different colors.
4	The trash can is empty.	The trash can is full.
5	There isn't paper in the printer.	There's paper in the printer.
6	There's a heater on the wall.	There isn't a heater on the wall.
7	There's a plant on the bookcase.	There isn't a plant on the bookcase.
8	The desk lamp is red.	The desk lamp is green.
9	There's a pocket calculator on the desk.	There isn't a pocket calculator on the desk.
10	There's a notepad on the desk and a pen on the notepad.	There's a notepad on the desk, but there isn't a pen.

2D Students work individually or in pairs and compare their answers with a partner or another pair. Go over the answers with the class.

Answer key

There are nine planets in the solar system.
There are ten countries in the ASEAN.
There are eleven players on a soccer team.
There are twenty-six letters in the English alphabet.
There are thirty-one days in January.

2 | Grammar focus
Focus 2: Adverbs of frequency

page 11

2E Play the first part of the recording again. Students complete sentences 1 and 2, compare their answers with a partner, and work together with the same partner to fill in the adverbs of frequency on the scale.

Answer key

1 You can **often** waste a lot of time . . .
2 There's **always** a lot of noise.

100%	*always*
	usually/normally
	often
	sometimes
	not often
0%	*never*

2F Adverbs of frequency are a lexical item, but their position in the sentence often causes problems. Ask students to look at the examples and underline the correct word to complete the rule.

Rule

Adverbs of frequency go **before** a full verb (*go, get, send . . .*), but **after** the verb *to be* and **after** *can, doesn't, don't*.

2G This task focuses on word order in sentences with adverbs of frequency. Students work in pairs to find the correct sentences, then compare their answers with another pair. Monitor the pairs. Go over the answers with the class.

Answer key

1 I don't often go to meetings.
2 Shaifful is never on time.
3 My colleagues are always helpful.
4 They don't often eat lunch in a restaurant.
5 Kamol always celebrates his birthday.
6 Hiroshi doesn't usually get many emails.
7 They always go on vacation in the summer.

2H This task gives students the opportunity for freer practice. See TIP 3 on pages xii–xiii for guidelines on pair work.

2I Students tell the class what they found out about their partner in 2H. In large classes, students can report to each other in groups. Your task is to monitor, prompt, and correct.

3 | Listening and speaking
A typical day

page 12

3A Before playing the recording, ask students to look at the pictures and the questions in the chart. Check comprehension. You may wish to pre-teach the key words at the bottom of page 12 as they will help students to understand the recording.

Follow Steps 2 to 7 of TIP 1 on page xi, with students working in pairs. Make sure students know that they should only write key words in the chart and remind them to listen for and note the adverbs of frequency. Ask them to report back in full sentences in the third person.

Example: *Cintya always gets up at seven o'clock. She gets to work at (about) nine-thirty.*

Answer key

Cintya always gets up at seven o'clock.
She gets to work at (about) nine-thirty.
First, she makes coffee, then she turns on the computer.
She usually has lunch at her desk.
She never travels on business.
In the evenings, she spends time with her two little children.

Mike usually gets up at six-thirty.
He gets to work at seven-thirty.
First, he has a meeting with his team, then he checks his email.
He always has lunch in the company cafeteria.
He travels a lot.
In the evenings, he often stays late in the office (for conference calls).

Kitty usually gets up at seven-thirty.
She always starts work at nine.
First, she checks in with her colleagues, then she goes to her computer to check her email/ then she checks her email.
She usually eats lunch with her colleagues in a café near the office.
She travels on business about three times a year.
She doesn't do a lot in the evenings because she's usually too tired.

3B This is the first *Talking about* . . . activity in the Student's Book. For guidelines see TIP 3 on pages xii–xiii. Your task is to monitor and prompt students at each step of the activity, and to give correction feedback at the end. The *Talking about* . . . activities work well in large classes as they involve individual, pair, and group work.

As an additional task for good students, you could give a student a role card with the name of a famous person. Other students interview the "famous person" and have to guess the name on the card. This can be done as a class or in groups.

4 Vocabulary focus
Focus 1: Office equipment

page 13

4A This task introduces some vocabulary for office equipment. Students work individually or in pairs and compare their answers with a partner or another pair. Go over the answers with the class (see illustrations).

4B This task practices simple prepositions. Students work individually or in pairs and compare their answers with a partner or another pair. Go over the answers with the class.

4C This task provides further practice of *there is* and *there are* and the prepositions from 4B. Example: *There's a computer on the desk. There are three pictures on the wall.*

4D This task provides further practice of the vocabulary introduced in 4A. See TIP 3 on pages xii–xiii for guidelines on pair work.

4 Vocabulary focus
Focus 2: Words that go together (1)

page 14

4E Tasks 4E to 4G practice word collocations. Play the recording. Students work individually or in pairs and compare their answers with a partner or another pair. Go over the answers with the class.

Answer key (exercise 4A)

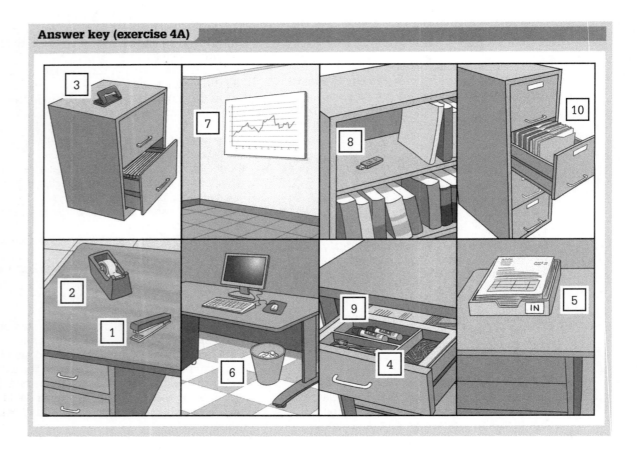

4F Follow the same procedure as in 4E.

Answer key

1 typical
2 sales
3 company
4 conference
5 main
6 starts
7 corner

4G Students work individually or in pairs and compare their answers with a partner or another pair. Go over the answers with the class.

Answer key

2 book
3 desk
4 night
5 morning
6 telephones
7 business
8 an email

4H The *Key words* task tests the vocabulary that is at the bottom of pages 9–12. This can be done as homework.

Answer key

1 breaks down
2 spend time
3 tired
4 midnight
5 noise
6 celebrate
7 sales manager
8 cafeteria

5 | **Reading**
Offices around the world

page 15

5A Encourage students to talk about the pictures. Ask them what they can see.

Possible answers

There is / There are chairs – tables – a big room – computers – people – basketball court – plants – bright colors . . .

5B Look at the guidelines on reading in TIP 2 on page xii. You may want to pre-teach some vocabulary, e.g., *education, environment, to choose, amazing, restroom, employee, atmosphere, advertising.*

Students work individually, then compare their answers with a partner. Go over the answers with the class.

Answer key

People who work for Mindvalley come from 31 different countries.
Fifteen people work in the Pons and Huot offices in Paris.
Google Ireland employees speak 46 different languages.
360 umbrellas hang from the ceiling of the Grupo Gallegos office.
Google Ireland employees come from 38 different countries.

5C Students work individually, then compare their answers with a partner. Go over the answers with the class.

Answer key

1 A Grupo Gallegos
  B Pons and Huot
  C Mindvalley

2 A Grupo Gallegos
  B Google Ireland
  C Mindvalley

5D In smaller classes students can tell the class which office they like best and why. In larger classes students can work in groups and tell each other their answers while you monitor and correct.

6 | **Business writing**
Emails

page 16

6A Students match the symbols and words in pairs, then compare their answers with other pairs. Go over the answers with the class.

Answer key

1 @   6 3
2 A   7 b
3 .   8 a
4 -   9 –
5 +

6B Students complete the email in pairs, then compare their answers with other pairs. Go over the answers with the class.

Answer key

1 To   5 Dear
2 From   6 Thank
3 Subject   7 attached
4 Attachment   8 Best regards

6C This task can be done in class or given as homework. In any case, it should be handed in for individual correction. In the next lesson, you can deal with any general problems and give remedial work to the class or individuals. Draw students' attention to the tip on page 16, which deals with opening and closing salutations.

TOEIC® practice (pages 17–18)

1 Listening

You will need to pause the recording between each task to give students time to think about and mark their answers.

1A Photographs

In this part of the test, students see a photograph and hear four statements (A–D) about the photograph. Students must choose the statement that best describes the photograph. In the test, the statements are not printed in the test book and are spoken only once, so students need to listen carefully.

However, for practice purposes you may wish to proceed as follows:

Students work as a class or in groups. Ask them to name everything they can see in the photograph. Put the words on the board. Then have students write sentences using some of the words. You might ask them to write a description of the photograph as homework.

When you feel that students have the vocabulary under control, they can do the listening task here and the speaking task in 2A.

Answer key

1 B	2 C

1B Question-Response

In this part of the test, students hear a question and three possible responses (A–C). Students must choose the best response to the question. In the test, the questions are not printed in the test book and will be spoken only once, so students need to listen carefully.

As many of the questions in this section begin with a question word, it is important that students can ultimately distinguish *who*, *what*, *when*, *where*, *why*, *how*, etc. For this task, focus on *how*, *who*, and *where*. For questions without question words, refer back to questions with *do/does* and *to be* in the *Grammar focus* in Unit 1 (pages 2–3).

A further useful practice strategy is to isolate the questions, e.g., *Can I help you with your bags?* Ask students who and where the speaker might be. Ask them to predict a possible correct response without looking at the distracters. Then do the listening task.

Answer key

1 C	2 A	3 B	4 C

2 Speaking

2A Describe a picture

In this part of the test, students describe a picture in as much detail as possible.

In the real test, students will have 30 seconds to prepare and 45 seconds to speak about the picture. For practice purposes this time can be extended. See also the practice strategies suggested in 1A.

Encourage students to ask themselves *who*, *what*, *where*, and *why* questions about the picture.

Who can I see? (number, gender, appearance)
What are they doing?
What can I see? (number, description of objects)
Where is / are . . . ? (location of people or things)

Why . . . ? (make assumptions about what you can see: *I think . . . , Perhaps . . . , It looks like . . .*)

Of course, students will need the present continuous tense to describe a picture properly. This will be dealt with in detail in Unit 3, so you may have to be a little tolerant of students' errors at this stage.

Possible answer to photograph 2

In the picture I can see three people meeting and greeting. There is a man on the left and a man and a woman on the right. I think the two people on the right are colleagues. They are all wearing formal clothes. They look like businesspeople. I think they are in an office. The man on the left is shaking hands with the woman on the right. I think it is their first meeting. Everyone is smiling. They look happy.

2B Read a text aloud

In this part of the test, students' pronunciation and intonation are tested. Students are given a text to read aloud. In the real test, students have 45 seconds to prepare and 45 seconds to read the text aloud. For practice purposes this time can be extended.

A useful practice strategy is to work together with your students to underline the words that a native speaker would normally stress, and to mark the place where a small pause (//) would be natural. Advise students to try not to read too fast.

Cintya Dewi is a <u>web</u> designer. // She works in the information technology <u>department</u> // of a big company in Jakarta. Cintya gets up at <u>seven</u> o'clock. // She goes to work by <u>car</u>. // It <u>takes</u> about an hour and a half. // She gets to the <u>office</u> at nine-thirty. // First she makes <u>coffee</u>, // then she turns on her <u>computer</u>. She doesn't eat <u>lunch</u> with her colleagues. // She usually has a <u>sandwich</u> at her desk. // She spends the <u>evenings</u> with her two little children.

3 Reading

Incomplete sentences

In this part of the test, students see sentences with a missing word or phrase.

Four answer choices (A–D) are given below each sentence. Students must choose the best answer to complete the sentences.

When practicing, give students time to complete the task, go over the answers with the class, then discuss wrong answers with them. It is important for them not only to know that an answer is wrong, but also why it is wrong.

The best way to learn reading comprehension is, of course, by reading. Students will also learn more vocabulary in context than from vocabulary lists. So encourage your students to try to read in English anything that interests them – online magazines, social networking sites, sports news, ads. The main thing is to read English, no matter what it is.

Answer key

1	D	4	B
2	B	5	D
3	C	6	C

4 Writing

Write a sentence based on a picture

In this part of the test, students are expected to show their mastery of grammar and vocabulary in a written sentence. Students write one sentence based on a picture. With the picture are two words or phrases that students must use. The forms of the words can be changed, and they can be used in any order.

Possible answer

1 The family always goes to the beach on weekends.
2 Tim often stays late at the office.

On the phone

Unit aims

In Unit 3 students will
- understand and use telephone phrases.
- learn to use the present continuous.
- learn to differentiate between present simple and present continuous.
- understand voicemail messages.
- discuss cell phones and their functions.
- spell names and say numbers.
- learn and use the International Telephone Alphabet (ITA).
- read about a new development in the world of cell phones.
- learn how to read a business card.
- read how to present a business card in different Asian countries.

Telephoning in a foreign language is notoriously difficult, but unavoidable in business and commerce. This unit covers some of the most typical expressions used on the phone in English and the use of the ITA in international business to spell names. It allows students to hear and practice the kind of language common to many business situations. Students will talk both on the telephone and about telephones.

The primary emphasis is, of course, on listening and speaking. The telephone conversations and voicemail messages are spoken by both native and non-native speakers.

 Business situation
Can I take a message?

page 19

1A Before playing the recording, look at the pictures. Explain that Hiroshi is making phone calls to his business partners. Tell students they will hear three phone calls. Follow Steps 2 to 5 of TIP 1 on page xi.

You may want to pre-teach the key words at the bottom of page 19 as they will help students understand the recording.

Answer key	
1	A
2	C
3	B

1B Ask students to read the expressions (1–10). Check comprehension. Ask students to listen and check the expressions they hear. Play the first one as an example. Students check Call 1. Continue the recording with students checking the phrases they hear. You will almost certainly have to play the recording at least twice before students have all the answers.

Students compare their answers with a partner, then go over the answers with the class. Follow Steps 6 and 7 of TIP 1 on page xi with students

working in pairs – although you might prefer not to let students see the script until they have completed 2A.

Answer key			
1	call 1	6	call 1
2	call 2	7	call 2
3	call 3	8	call 1
4	call 1	9	call 1
5	call 2	10	call 1

 Grammar focus
Present simple and present continuous

pages 20–21

2A Play the recording again. Students fill in the missing words and compare their answers with a partner. Go over the answers with the class.

Answer key
1 Mr. Neo **is talking** on the other line at the moment.
2 They **are having** lunch.
3 Greg: I'm/I **am looking** at the new designs right now.

2B Using the examples in 2A, guide students to complete the rule.

Rule

The present continuous is formed with the verb *to be* + the *-ing* form of the verb.

To introduce the short forms, you could write the following chart on the board and have students help you to fill it in, then copy it into their notebooks. Point out that long forms are used in writing – especially in formal texts such as business letters – and short forms are used in conversation. This is mentioned briefly in the tip at the bottom of page 21.

to be	short form	*-ing*
I am	I'm	
He/she/it is	He's/she's/it's	
We/you/they are	We're/you're/they're	sleeping.

2C Students work individually or in pairs and compare their answers with a partner or another pair. Go over the answers with the class.

Possible answers

2 Kasem is sitting in the office.
3 Mai is Skyping with a friend.
4 The cat is sleeping/lying on the keyboard.
5 We are playing computer games.
6 The colleagues are having a meeting/are sleeping at the meeting.

Note: You can introduce the short answers with a quick question-answer session based on task 2C. Put these short answers on the board first, then ask the questions below.

Yes, I am.	*No, I'm not.*
Yes, he is.	*No, he isn't.*
Yes, she is.	*No, she isn't.*
Yes, it is.	*No, it isn't.*
Yes, we are.	*No, we aren't.*
Yes, they are.	*No, they aren't.*

Am I having lunch?
Am I having breakfast?

Is Kasem working in his office?
Is he in the cafeteria?

Is Mai Skyping?
Is she reading a book?

Is the cat sleeping?
Is it playing in the garden?

Are we sitting on the train?
Are we working in the office?

Are the colleagues sleeping?
Are they working hard?

2D Put students in pairs and ask Student A not to look at the information on this page, but to go straight to Partner file 2 on page 92. When you are certain that students have understood the instructions, start the activity. See TIP 3 on pages xii–xiii for further guidelines on pair work.

2E Focus students' attention on the sentences and guide them to complete the rule. **Note:** The use of the present continuous for future plans is covered in Unit 5.

Rule

We use the **present continuous** to talk about things that are happening now.
We use the **present simple** to talk about things that often happen.

Draw students' attention to the tip about the "double do" on page 21.

You may want to practice the short answers in the present simple using the information in 2E.

Write on the board:
Yes, I/you/we/they do.   No, I/you/we/they don't.
Yes, he/she/it does.   No, he/she/it doesn't.

Ask:
Does Hiroshi usually work late?
Does Hiroshi always work on his wife's birthday?
Do Hiroshi and Greg often have lunch together?
Do Hiroshi and Greg always have lunch alone?
Does Anocha sometimes write an email to her boss?
Does Anocha write emails every evening?

2F Students work individually or in pairs and compare their answers with a partner or another pair. Go over the answers with the class.

Answer key

2 A: Can I speak to Mr. Young? I **am** / I'm **calling** about the new course.
   B: No, sorry, he **is** / he's **talking** to another student at the moment. Can you call back later?
3 A: Listen! **Is your phone ringing?**
   B: Yes. I **am**/ I'm **expecting** a call from my parents. They **always call** me on Sundays.
4 Mai **usually leaves** the office at five o'clock. Now it is five o'clock, but Mai **is not** / **isn't leaving** the office. She **is** / She's **staying** longer today.
5 **Are they attending** the conference in Hawaii this week?
6 A: What **are you working** on at the moment?
   B: I **am** / I'm **preparing** a presentation for the next lesson.
7 Christine is on a business trip in Osaka. She **is** / She's **enjoying** the trip. She **always enjoys** her trips to Osaka.

Note: You can use the pictures in 2C again to get some extra practice.

1 *What is the man doing?*
Where does he usually have lunch?
2 *What is Kasem doing?*
Does he . . . every day?
3 *What is Mai doing?*
How often does she . . . ?
4 *What is the cat doing?*
How long does it usually . . . ?
5 *What are the people doing?*
Do they . . . every morning?
6 *What are the colleagues doing?*
Do they always do that in meetings?

3 Listening and speaking
On the phone

page 22

3A The introduction to the task sets the scene. Follow Steps 2 to 6 of TIP 1 on page xi. Finally, you can have students read the script aloud. Correct pronunciation and intonation on the spot.

Note: Telephone numbers are read as individual numbers with a short pause between groups of numbers, so sentence 5 will be spoken as *zero one zero // six five // eight six five three // one seven two eight.*

Answer key

1 Greg wants to meet for lunch at twelve (*not* one-thirty).
2 Please call back this afternoon (*not* this morning).
3 Takeshi wants to meet in front of his office (*not* in his office).
4 Please call Ms. Klein back (*not* she will call back).
5 The number is 010 65 8653 1728. (*not* 1827).
6 The company can't send the equipment until next month (*not* they can't send it next month).

3B Here students have the opportunity to talk about their cell phones and the functions that are important to them. For guidelines on *Talking about . . .* activities, see TIP 3 on pages xii–xiii. Your task is to monitor and prompt students at each step of the activity, and to give correction feedback at the end.

4 Vocabulary focus
Focus 1: Spelling names and saying numbers

page 23

4A Some students will be familiar with the letters of the alphabet and others less so. Before listening ask students to go through the alphabet. In weaker classes, you may want to act as a role model. Then tell students they will hear four people spelling their names. Follow Steps 2 to 5 of TIP 1 on page xi, with students working in pairs.

Answer key

1 Rozita
2 Yeonyi
3 Shirley
4 Jerri

4B Tell students that they will hear the International Telephone Alphabet, which is used by businesspeople all over the world. Play the recording once. Then play it again and have students repeat each letter. Students can work in pairs or groups and test each other by calling out a letter, e.g., "M"; their partner has to say "Mike." Further practice can be integrated into any lesson. When students hear new names, you can ask: *How do you think we spell . . . ?*

4C Tell students they will hear some more people spelling their names, but this time with the help of the ITA. Follow Steps 2 to 6 in TIP 1 on page xi.

Answer key

1 Yori Sanada
2 Miki Nomura
3 Tom Robbins
4 Paresh Vartak
5 Jin Woong
6 Quentin F(rank) Lopez

Finally, you can have students read the script aloud. Correct pronunciation and intonation on the spot.

4D This pair work task can be done several times with different partners. See suggestions for organizing pair and group work in TIP 3 on pages xii–xiii.

4E Clarify the vocabulary with students and draw attention to the tip at the bottom of page 23 on the use of *zero* and *oh*. Have students work in pairs to fill in the missing words. Go over the answers with the class, then students work in pairs to ask and answer the two questions. Your task is to monitor the pairs and correct on the spot. See the note on reading telephone numbers in 3A.

Answer key

+ 61 is the country code
(0)3 is the area code
1234567 is the subscriber number
21 is the extension number

4 Vocabulary focus
Focus 2: Telephone language
page 24

4F This task reinforces the use of the telephone phrases encountered in the Business Situation. Students work individually or in pairs and compare their answers with a partner or another pair. Go over the answers with the class.

Answer key

1	repeat	6	back
2	help	7	call
3	through	8	possible
4	leave	9	message
5	line		

4G Students work in pairs. They can use their cell phones and pretend the conversation is real. Follow the guidelines on pair work in TIP 3 on pages xii–xiii.

4H The *Key words* task tests the vocabulary that is at the bottom of pages 19–22. This can be done as homework.

Answer key

1 repeat
2 right now . . . call back
3 at the moment . . . take . . . message
4 attends
5 equipment
6 battery
7 expects
8 client

5 Reading
The unbreakable cell phone
page 25

5A Students work in pairs and answer the questions. You can ask some of the most confident students with an interesting story to tell it to the class.

5B Look at the guidelines on reading in TIP 2 on page xii. You may wish to pre-teach some of the vocabulary, e.g., *to develop, development, to discover, amazing, screen*.

Students work individually, then compare their answers with a partner. Go over the answers with the class.

Answer key

1 Not correct. The material we have in our pencils is graphite.
2 Not correct. Two scientists discovered it.
3 Not correct. It was discovered in 2004.
4 Correct.
5 Not correct. It is cheaper than the material we are using at the moment.
6 Not correct. Nokia and IBM are looking at different uses.

5C Students read the text again more slowly and look for the answers to the two questions. They can compare their answers with a partner. Go over the answers with the class.

Answer key

1 The Nobel Prize for Physics, because graphene is an amazing material.
2 Smartphone users touch their screens hundreds of times a day.

5D Now students can talk about their own phones. See the guidelines on pair work in TIP 3 on pages xii–xiii.

6A Ask students not to look at page 26, but first to think about the kind of information they would expect to see on a business card (the person's name, job title, company name, address, phone number, email address). Then have students work in pairs to label the business card. They can compare their answers with other pairs. Go over the answers with the class.

In addition, you can revise the vocabulary from 4E by asking students to look at the telephone number and say which is the country code, area code, and subscriber number. See the note on reading telephone numbers in 3A.

6B You may want to pre-teach some vocabulary, e.g., *to present, nod, immediately, impolite.*

Students should read the text individually first, then work with a partner to answer the questions. Then partners compare their answers with another pair. Go over the answers with the class. Have students take turns reading the text aloud.

Answer key

1 China and Japan
2 India and other Islamic countries.
3 It is acceptable to put the card away immediately.
4 *Answers will vary.*

Answer key

Buying and selling

Unit aims

In Unit 4 students will
- listen to and understand conversations in a store.
- ask and answer questions with *some* and *any*, *much*, and *many*.
- discuss shopping habits and the service in stores.
- practice understanding and giving directions.
- learn and use more word collocations.
- read about a modern way of shopping.
- write a business inquiry.
- practice listening, speaking, reading, and writing for the TOEIC® test.

As the title suggests, this unit focuses mainly on the topics of buying and selling, but it also includes practice for understanding and giving directions, and the opportunity to write a business inquiry.

Getting lower-level students to talk is never easy, but as our aim is to have a classroom in which students speak much more than the teacher, it is essential to build students' confidence by giving them as much encouragement as possible to talk about things they know. As all students will have had some experience of shopping, they should be comfortable with the topics in this unit, and willing and able to talk about their own experience during the communication activities. In addition, it takes the pressure off you, the teacher, if students are motivated to talk to you and each other, and communicate their own thoughts and ideas in English.

 1 **Business situation**
Helping customers

page 27

1A Before playing the recording, put the following questions on the board. Students ask and answer the questions in pairs. Ask for feedback.
Who are the two people in the picture? (customer and store clerk)
What kind of store is it? (computer store, telephone store)
What kind of things can you buy there? (computers, cell phones, tablets, etc.)
How is the customer paying? (with a/by credit card)

Tell students they will hear three conversations between a store clerk and his customers. You may want to pre-teach the key words at the bottom of pages 27 and 29 as they will help students understand the recording.

Follow Steps 2 to 5 of TIP 1 on page xi for each conversation. Draw students' attention to the pronunciation of the weak form *some* /səm/.

When all three conversations have been dealt with, you can follow Steps 6 and 7 with students working in pairs, although you might prefer not to let students see the script until they have completed 2A.

Answer key

1	A
2	C
3	C
4	B
5	B
6	A

2 **Grammar focus**
Focus 1: *some* and *any*

page 28

We use *some* and *any* when we don't know the exact number. The rule that *some* is used in positive sentences and *any* in questions and negatives is not quite true – the tip on page 28 indicates this – but it is still useful at this level.

2A Play the recording again. Students work individually to complete the sentences, then compare their answers with a partner. Go over the answers with the class.

2B Using the examples in 2A, guide students to complete the rule.

Rule

We use **some** in positive statements.
We use **any** in negative statements.
We use **any** in questions.

2C Students work individually or in pairs and compare their answers with a partner or another pair. Go over the answers with the class.

2D Put students in pairs and ask Student A not to look at the information on this page, but to go straight to Partner file 3 on page 92. When you are certain that students have understood the instructions, start the activity. See TIP 3 on pages xii–xiii for further guidelines on pair work.

If you want additional practice, you can revise *there is* and *there are* by asking students to complete these sentences about the classroom, using *some* and *any*:
In our classroom there is . . . , but there isn't . . .
In our classroom there are . . . , but there aren't . . .
Students can also write similar sentences about their homes.

2 Grammar focus
Focus 2: *much* and *many*

page 29

2E Focus students' attention on the sentences from the conversations. Ask them to decide in pairs which word to underline to complete the rule. They can compare their answers with another pair before you go over the answers with the class.

Rule

We use *much* with **singular** words.
We use *many* with **plural** words.

2F Follow the guidelines on pair work in TIP 3 on pages xii–xiii. Make sure students interview lots of different partners. This task is tightly controlled as students would be overtaxed at this stage if confronted with the additional rule that *much* is not normally used is positive statements. **I drink much coffee.*

Draw students' attention to the tip on page 29. We can use *a lot of* with both singular and plural words, but students will need to learn *much* and *many* to use the questions *how much* and *how many* correctly.

page 30

3A Before playing the recording, encourage students to talk about the pictures. Ask them what they see. In bigger classes you can ask students to work in pairs and describe the pictures to each other.

Ask: How do you think Liu and Huan like to shop?

Possible answers

Liu likes to shop in real stores / in the shopping mall.
Huan prefers to shop online.

3B Follow Steps 2 to 5 of TIP 1 on page xi. You may want to pre-teach the key words at the bottom of page 30 as they will help students to understand the recording.

Answer key

1 They go from store to store and compare prices.
   They experiment with styles.
   They try things on.
   They take breaks for ice cream and coffee.
2 It's boring.
   You can't see and feel things.
   You can't see the quality of the product.
   You need a lot of time to pack things up and send them back.
   It's easy to spend too much money.
3 It's boring.
   It's hectic and busy.
   You waste a lot of time just to get there.
4 It is quicker/faster (to go from website to website than from store to store).
   You can save money (because it's easy to compare prices).
   There's better information about electronic equipment.
   There are more choices.

3C Follow Steps 2 to 5 of TIP 1 on page xi.

Answer key

1 Not correct. She goes with her friends.
2 Not correct. She never shops online.
3 Correct.
4 Not correct. He knows what he likes.

Finally, play the recording again while students follow the script. You can have students read the script aloud. Correct pronunciation and intonation on the spot.

3D Here students have the opportunity to talk about their own experience. For guidelines on *Talking about . . .* activities, see TIP 3 on pages xii–xiii. Your task is to monitor and prompt students at each step of the activity, and to give correction feedback at the end.

page 31

4A Tell students that they will hear a conversation on the street. Play the first sentence of the recording and ask, *What is the person looking for?* (Answer: the restrooms). Read the instructions to your students, then follow Steps 3 to 5 of TIP 1 on page xi.

Answer key

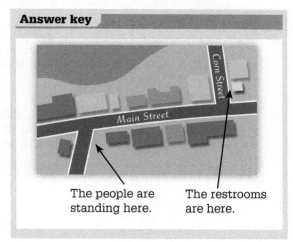

The people are standing here.   The restrooms are here.

4B Follow Steps 2 to 6 of TIP 1 on page xi. As the conversation is very short, it is hardly worth organizing pair work for Step 7. You can simply ask students to read the conversation aloud. Correct pronunciation and intonation on the spot.

Answer key

1 straight
2 right
3 left
4 next to . . . opposite

4C This task gives students further practice in understanding directions. Tell students they will hear Liu telling her friend how to get to a store called Alta Moda. Point out Alta Moda on the map. Follow Steps 2 to 6 of TIP 1 on page xi. Finally, you can have students read the script aloud. Correct pronunciation and intonation on the spot.

4D This task gives students free practice in giving directions. Look at TIP 3 on pages xii–xiii for guidelines on pair work. Make sure students work with a lot of different partners.

4 Vocabulary focus
Focus 2: Words that go together (2)
page 32

This section gives students further practice in word collocations. The individual words should already be familiar to students, so they can focus fully on the collocations.

4E Students work individually or in pairs and compare their answers with a partner or another pair. Go over the answers with the class.

4F Students work individually or in pairs and compare their answers with a partner or another pair. Go over the answers with the class.

4G Students work individually or in pairs and compare their answers with a partner or another pair. Go over the answers with the class.

4H The *Key words* task tests the vocabulary that is at the bottom of pages 27–30. This can be done as homework.

5 Reading
Showrooming
page 33

5A You will need to explain that "showrooming" is a new word that students might not find in their dictionaries. It means visiting a store to look at things or try things on, then go home and buy the item online at a lower price.

5B Look at the guidelines on reading in TIP 2 on page xii. Pre-teaching vocabulary should not be necessary for this article. Students work individually, then compare their answers with a partner. Go over the answers with the class.

5C Students should work individually, then compare their answers with a partner. Go over the answers with the class.

5D Students now have the opportunity to talk about themselves in class, groups, or pairs. If students have worked in groups and pairs, you can ask some students to tell the class about their partner or another student in their group, thus maximizing student talking time.

6 Business writing
An inquiry

page 34

Read the instructions and have students read the Robotbird advertisement. Check comprehension.

Ask students to look again at the business email they wrote on page 16 in Unit 2. The model email will help students fulfill the task on page 34. Guide students orally through the prompts, then set the written task in class or as homework. In any case, it should be handed in for individual correction. In the next lesson, you can deal with any general problems and give remedial work to the class or individuals.

Draw students' attention to the tip at the bottom of page 34, which deals with the subject line of an email.

TOEIC® practice (pages 35–36)

1 Listening

You will need to pause the recording between each task to give students time to think about and mark their answers.

1A Photographs

In this part of the test, students see a photograph and hear four statements (A–D) about the photograph. Students must choose the statement that best describes the photograph. In the test, the statements are not printed in the test book and are spoken only once, so students need to listen carefully.

For teaching and practice tips for this part of the test, see the notes to Unit 2 TOEIC® practice 1A on page 12.

Answer key	
1 C	2 D

1B Conversations

In this part of the test, students hear some short conversations between two people. Students see and hear three questions on each conversation. There are four possible answers (A–D). Students have to choose the correct answer.

In the test, the conversations are not printed in the test book and are spoken only once, so students need to listen carefully.

In the real test, students have eight seconds to answer each question. You might want to proceed more slowly in the practice phase. The questions in this section ask for specific information such as a price, a day, a time, or a person's job. They begin with a question word, so it is important that students can distinguish *who*, *what*, *when*, *where*, *why*, *how*, *which*, etc.

Encourage students to scan the questions before the recording begins in order to see what kind of information they have to listen for.

Answer key			
Conversation 1		**Conversation 2**	
1 D		1 B	
2 D		2 A	
3 C		3 D	

2 Speaking

Describe a picture

In this part of the test, students describe a picture in as much detail as possible.

In the real test, students will have 30 seconds to prepare and 45 seconds to speak about the picture. For practice purposes this time can be extended. See also the tips and strategies suggested in Unit 2 TOEIC® practice 1A and 2A on pages 12–13.

> **Possible answer to photograph 2**
>
> There are two people in the photograph; on the left there is a young man and on the right a young woman. They look like students. Behind them there are a lot of books on bookshelves. I think the people are in a library. Perhaps it's the college library. The girl is carrying a lot of books. They look very heavy. I think it is difficult for her to hold the books. The boy is trying to help her.

3 Reading

Text completion

In this part of the test, students see a text (e.g., email, article, advertisement, notice) with some words and phrases missing in some of the sentences. Four answer choices (A–D) are given below the sentences. Students have to select the best answer to complete the text.

The same practice strategies apply here as in the section *Incomplete sentences* in Unit 2 TOEIC® practice 3 on page 13.

Answer key			
1 D	2 A	3 B	4 C

4 Writing

Respond to a written request

In this part of the test, students show how well they can write a reply to an email. The reply will be scored on the quality and variety of the grammatical structures and vocabulary, as well as on the organization of the email and the correct use of email conventions. In the real test, students have ten minutes to read and answer each email. For practice purposes this time can be extended. Remind students to read the email carefully before they write their replies.

For this part of the test, it is important that students know the correct forms of salutation in emails. This is dealt with in *Business writing* in Unit 2. There is further practice in email writing in Units 4, 6, 8, and 10.

What are you doing tomorrow?

Unit aims

In Unit 5 students will
- learn and use the present continuous to talk about future plans.
- understand a discussion about making plans for the future.
- learn and practice how to make suggestions.
- practice days, months, dates, and times.
- learn to use prepositions with days, dates, and times.
- exchange opinions on train and air travel.
- learn about communication styles in different countries.
- talk about communication styles in their country.

The main focus of this unit is on making plans and arrangements for the future, using the present continuous tense with days, dates, and times.

The unit starts with a conversation between John Santos, Dr. Mark Little's assistant, and David Parks, who is at a conference in Manila and wishes to meet Dr. Little. This conversation is one of many in the Student's Book where native and non-native English speakers communicate. The native speaker's utterances in the recordings can serve each time as models for students' pronunciation, intonation, and word and sentence stress. Although there are no activities in the Student's Book aimed specifically at improving pronunciation, getting students to copy these models is a relatively easy way to help them to produce English that is clear and understandable.

When introducing new vocabulary items, always make sure that students learn the correct word stress. Show them how they can recognize word stress in dictionary entries, and how they can mark word stress in their vocabulary books. The phonetic script uses the stress mark ', e.g., /'dɪkʃənri:/, but students may feel more comfortable marking the word stress like this: ● ● ●
dictionary.

1 Business situation
Making an appointment

`page 37`

 1A Before playing the recording, ask students to tell you who they sometimes have appointments with (e.g., a doctor, dentist, bank manager). Point out the difference between *an appointment* (a formal arrangement to meet) and *a date* (an informal arrangement to meet friends, especially a romantic meeting). Ask students where they record their appointments – iCal, pocket agenda, wall calendar.

Tell students they will hear a phone call between John Santos, who works in Manila, and David Parks, who is attending a conference in Manila. You may want to pre-teach the key words at the bottom of page 37 as they will help students understand the recording.

Follow Steps 1 to 7 of TIP 1 on page xi, with students working in pairs. After the listening task, you can use parts of the conversation to practice pronunciation, as suggested in the introduction to this unit.

John:	John Santos, Greencheck Software. How can I help you?
Mr. Parks:	Can I speak to Dr. Little, please? My name's David Parks. Dr. Little and I were in **Hong Kong** at a conference last week. This week I'm in Manila. Dr. Little is expecting my call.
John:	I'm sorry, Mr. Parks. He's in a meeting right now, but he wants me to make an appointment with you.
Mr. Parks:	Fine. Can you make a suggestion?
John:	Let me see, mmm, today's **Tuesday**. Is later today possible?
Mr. Parks:	No, sorry. I'm having lunch with a client at **one o'clock**, and later today I am attending a workshop. What about tomorrow?
John:	I'm sorry. Dr. Little has a lot of **meetings** on Wednesday. Let's look at Thursday.
Mr. Parks:	No, no. On Thursday I'm meeting some **clients**. What about the day after?
John:	Friday is no problem. What's better for you, the morning or the afternoon?
Mr. Parks:	The morning is better for me.
John:	Well, why don't you come late morning, Mr. Parks? Then you can have **lunch** with Dr. Little.
Mr. Parks:	That's a good idea. Shall we say eleven-thirty?
John:	Fine. Friday at eleven-thirty. Thank you for your call. Goodbye.

2 Grammar focus
Present continuous for future plans
[pages 38–39]

2A Students work in pairs to find the correct answers, then compare their answers with another pair. Go over the answers with the class.

He's in a meeting right now.	**Present**
Later today I'm attending a workshop.	**Future**
On Thursday I'm meeting some clients.	**Future**

Use the examples from 2A to guide students to complete the rule.

At this point, you can also draw their attention to the tip on page 38: *"We also use the present continuous just before you do something in the future."*

Rule

We can use the present continuous in two ways:
1 to talk about **the present**.
2 to talk about **the future**.

2B Students work in pairs to find the correct answers, then compare their answers with another pair. Monitor the pairs. Go over the answers with the class.

1	F	4	P
2	P	5	P
3	F	6	F

2C Students work individually or in pairs and compare their answers with a partner or another pair. Go over the answers with the class.

2 Who is Mr. Parks meeting for lunch tomorrow?
3 Are you going out tonight?
4 When are you seeing Huan again?
5 Where is John going on vacation next year?
6 Are Lan and Diu playing tennis next Sunday morning?

2D Students work in pairs and take turns to ask and answer questions about future plans. Monitor the pairs.

2E Put students in pairs and ask Student A not to look at the information on this page, but to go straight to Partner file 4 on page 93. Tell students they should take turns to ask and answer questions to complete the agenda. When you are certain that students have understood the instructions, start the activity. See TIP 3 on pages xii–xiii for further guidelines on pair work.

B: What time is he arriving in London on Tuesday?
A: He's arriving at ten AM.
A: Where is he staying (for two nights) on Tuesday and Wednesday?
B: He's staying in King's Hotel.
B: Who is he meeting at ten-thirty AM on Wednesday?
A: He's meeting David Johnson.
A: What time is he having lunch with Marion Smith on Thursday?
B: He's having lunch with her at twelve-thirty PM.
B: When is he taking the train to Liverpool on Thursday?
A: He's taking the train at three PM.
A: Which hotel is he staying at/in in Liverpool on Thursday?
B: He's staying in the Mersey Hotel.
B: What is he doing at ten AM on Friday?
A: He's attending a workshop.
A: What time is he leaving Liverpool / flying back to Manila on Friday?
B: He's leaving Liverpool / flying back to Manila at six PM.
B: When is he arriving in Manila on Saturday?
A: He's arriving at eleven PM.

Plans for this week

Thursday 10 AM	Lien, Huan, and Ken are having a meeting about the band's **promotion campaign**.
Friday 2 PM	Lien is meeting **the band's agent**.

Plans for next week

Tuesday 5 PM	The band is coming to the office to **sign the contract**.
Tuesday 7 PM	The band, their agent, and Lien's team are having **dinner** at **a restaurant** called Amigo.
Wednesday 8 AM	The band is recording in **the studio**.
Friday	Ken **is meeting** the designer, and she **is bringing** some cover designs with her.

3B Play the recording again. Follow Steps 2 to 5 of TIP 1 on page xi.

Let's check the plans. *Let's* make sure they're back in their hotel before ten.
Would it be possible for me to come, too?
What about trying that new restaurant?
Why don't you book a table for eight at 7 PM?
Should we have a meeting about that the day after tomorrow?

After the feedback for 3B, play the recording again. Follow Steps 6 and 7 of TIP 1 on page xi, with students working in groups of three. See TIP 3 on pages xii–xiii for guidelines on group work.

3 Listening and speaking
Making plans and suggestions

page 40

3A Before playing the recording, ask students to look at the picture and the instructions.

Ask: *Where does Lien Hu work? How many people are on her team? What are they discussing?*
You may want to pre-teach the key words at the bottom of page 40 as they will help students to understand the recording.

Follow Steps 2 to 5 of TIP 1 on page xi. As the information required to complete the sentences does not occur chronologically in the script, it may be necessary to play the recording several times in Step 3.

3C Students work in groups of three and make suggestions for situations 1–6. Monitor the groups. Prompt and correct while students are working. One of the group can take notes. As feedback, ask one group for their suggestions to, for example, situation 1, then ask the other groups if they have any different suggestions.

Vocabulary focus
Focus 1: Days, months, dates
page 41

Introduce the topic by asking: *What day is it today? What is the date today?*

4A Play the recording at least twice. Students listen and repeat in chorus. Then individual students say the names of the days without the model. This can be done as a chain exercise, i.e., the first student says *Monday*, the second student says *Tuesday*, and so on around the class. When you are satisfied with students' pronunciation, move on to task 4B.

4B Same procedure as in 4A. Look out for difficulties with the pronunciation of February /ˈfebrʊərɪ/.

4C Listen to the recording and have students repeat the dates, at first in chorus and then individually. Draw attention to the tip on page 41. Tell students to write down five dates the American way, and their partner will say the dates. Monitor the pairs. If you feel students need more practice on dates, do a birthday survey.

4D Play the recording at least twice. Students compare their answers with a partner. Go over the answers with the class.

Answer key	
1 A: June 1	B: July 1
2 A: Monday	B: Tuesday . . . Wednesday
3 A: February	B: March 22
4 B: October 30	

4E Focus students' attention on the prepositions + time. Students can do the task individually or in pairs. Go over the answers with the class.

Answer key					
1	In	3	In	5	On
2	on	4	At	6	At

4F See TIP 3 on pages xii–xiii for guidelines on pair work. Make sure students work with lots of different partners.

Vocabulary focus
Focus 2: Telling the time
page 42

4G Introduce the topic by asking: *What time is it now? What time does this lesson finish?* Ask students to listen and number the times in the order that they hear them. First play the example, then play the recording twice. Go over the answers with the class.

Get students to practice saying the times using the recording or yourself as a model. Draw attention to the tip on page 42 and explain that the 24-hour clock (e.g., 16:30) is generally only used in schedules (e.g., for trains and airplanes). You can also have students draw clock faces and ask their partner to tell the time.

Answer key	
05:30	6
14:45	2
07:35	1
15:30	4
08:20	8
18:40	3
11:15	5
20:45	9
12:00	10
19:00	7

4H See TIP 3 on pages xii–xiii for guidelines on pair work. Make sure students work with lots of different partners.

4I Students can work in pairs or small groups. They should make one sentence about each of the cities on the map (seven sentences). If you want students to be more accurate, you can put words such as *about, nearly, just after* on the board. Have them compare their answers with another pair. Go over the answers with the class.

Possible answers
When it's four AM in Los Angeles, it's (about) nine PM in Tokyo.
When it's (just after) seven AM in New York, it's (nearly) eleven PM in Sydney.
When it's nine AM in Rio de Janeiro, it's (nearly) four PM in Riyadh.
When it's noon in London, it's (just before) ten PM in Tokyo.
When it's four PM in Riyadh, it's three AM in Los Angeles.
When it's (nearly) ten PM in Tokyo, it's (about) nine-thirty AM in Rio die Janeiro.
When it's eleven PM in Sydney, it's (just after) seven AM in New York.

4J The *Key words* task tests the vocabulary that is at the bottom of pages 37–40. This can be done as homework.

Answer key

1 noon
2 necessary
3 worry about
4 agenda
5 business trip
6 agent . . . contract
7 improve
8 suggestion

5 Reading
London to Beijing in two days

page 43

5A Students work in pairs. See TIP 3 on pages xii–xiii for guidelines on pair work. In the feedback phase, you can put a chart on the board and ask students to write in key words.

Travel by train		Travel by air	
Good	Not so good	Good	Not so good

5B Before reading you might like to pre-teach some of the vocabulary, e.g., *passenger*, *rail network*, *mph* (= *miles per hour*), *to connect*, *link*. Look at the guidelines on reading in TIP 2 on page xii. Students work individually, then compare their answers with a partner. Go over the answers with the class.

Answer key

2	As fast as airplanes	A
3	The world's fastest train	E
4	5,000 miles in two days	C
5	Linking South East Asia	D

5C Students work individually or in pairs and compare their answers with a partner or another pair. Go over the answers with the class.

Answer key

1 London to Beijing: two days
   London to Singapore: three days
2 London to Beijing: 5,000 miles
   Beijing to Singapore: 6,750 miles
3 1) a high-speed rail network in India and Europe
   2) trains that go south to connect Vietnam, Thailand, Myanmar, and Malaysia
   3) high-speed lines to connect all of China's major cities
4 It is a very old line built by the French in Vietnam a hundred years ago.
5 1) Its name is Harmony Express.
   2) It has a top speed of nearly 250 mph.
   3) It runs between the cities of Wuhan and Guangzhou.

 5D Students answer the questions in pairs. See TIP 3 on pages xii–xiii for guidelines on pair work. Finally, depending on the size of the class, you can ask all or some students: *Does your partner enjoy traveling by train? Why (not)?*

6 Culture focus
Communication styles

page 44

6A Before you listen, ask students what they can see in the pictures.

Answer key

Australia: Sydney Opera House
China: Great Wall of China
Germany: Brandenburg Gate, Berlin

Ask students what they know about the three countries – even if you can only elicit a few words, this helps to set the scene. Tell students they will hear an Australian expert talking about international communication styles. Follow Steps 2 to 5 of TIP 1 on page xi. After the feedback phase, follow Step 6. Finally, you can have students read the script aloud. Correct pronunciation and intonation on the spot.

Which country?	Australia	China	Germany
1 People have no problem with the word "no."	✔		✔
2 It is important to watch a person's body language.		✔	
3 Businesspeople are formal.		✔	✔
4 It is usual to use first names with business partners.	✔		
5 It is OK to interrupt people in meetings.	✔		✔
6 Businesspeople don't feel comfortable with small talk.			✔
7 People like working in teams.	✔	✔	

6B Students work in small groups or pairs to find the correct answers, then compare their answers with another group or pair. Go over the answers with the class. Ask students why they chose their answers. For this students can refer back to the script.

Example for 1: *We think an Australian said this. When the Australians say "no," they also say "I'm sorry."*

Answer key

1 A	4 G	7 A, G
2 C	5 A, C	
3 A	6 G	

6C Students work in groups and talk about communication styles in their country. See TIP 3 on pages xii–xiii for guidelines on pair work.

Out and about

Unit aims

In Unit 6 students will
- play the role of a hotel reservations clerk.
- use comparative and superlative adjectives to compare people, places, and things.
- listen to a speaker giving advice.
- talk about different types of vacation.
- discuss ways of traveling.
- learn how to describe pictures.
- read and understand comments on a hotel.
- write a confirmation of a hotel reservation.
- practice listening, speaking, reading, and writing for the TOEIC® test.

This unit examines the vocabulary needed for business travel and traveling for pleasure. It introduces comparative and superlative adjectives and gives students an opportunity to learn and practice describing pictures – a skill required in the TOEIC® tests.

As this unit contains a lot of new vocabulary, it is a good moment to talk to your students about using a dictionary to solve many of their learning problems. Make students aware of the fact that a dictionary shows not only the spelling and meaning of words, but also explains the grammar (e.g., singular or plural) and the use of the word in context. It tells us what part of speech (noun, verb, adjective, etc.) a word is, and where the main word stress lies. Ask students:
When and why do you look up words?
What information can you find about a word?

Together with the class, look up some simple words from the unit such as *travel* and *hotel* and discover what information can be found there. Students can then work in groups to make further dictionary discoveries.

1 Business situation
Customer service in a hotel
page 45

 Before playing the recording, ask students, What does a hotel reservations clerk do? (*She answers the phone, makes and changes reservations, and confirms bookings.*)

You may want to pre-teach the key words at the bottom of page 45 as they will help students understand the recording. Play both conversations once (twice if necessary). Students work in pairs to complete the sentences. Go over the answers with the class.

Answer key

Conversation 1: The caller wants to **stay longer / for two more nights**.

Conversation 2: The caller informs the hotel that **he is arriving late / later / at twelve-thirty the latest**.

1B The conversations can be dealt with one at a time, following Steps 2 to 5 of TIP 1 on page xi each time. For conversation 1 answer questions 1 to 4, for conversation 2 questions 5 to 8. In more advanced classes, you can have students match the sentence parts before they listen, and then listen and check.

Answer key

Conversation 1	Conversation 2
1 F	5 C
2 G	6 H
3 A	7 B
4 E	8 D

Finally, follow Steps 6 and 7 of TIP 1 on page xi, with students working in pairs, although you might prefer not to let students see the script until they have completed 2A.

1C Put students in pairs and ask Student A not to look at the information on this page, but to go straight to Partner file 5 on page 93. When you are certain that students have understood the instructions, start the activity. See TIP 3 on pages xii–xiii for further guidelines on pair work.

2 Grammar focus
Comparing people, places, and things
pages 46–47

The use of the *-er/-est* endings for short adjectives and *more/most* with long adjectives is introduced here, as well as the irregular *good – better – best* and *bad – worse – worst*. The use of *-ier/-iest* endings with adjectives that end in y (e.g., *happy – happier – happiest*) is not introduced at this stage, but with more advanced students you can give them this information after 2B or 2C, using the classroom environment with examples such as:

heavy – heavier – the heaviest book
noisy – noisier – the noisiest student/class
friendly – friendlier – the friendliest teacher
easy – easier – the easiest exercise

2A Play conversation 1 from 1A again. Students work in pairs to complete the sentences, then compare their answers with another pair. Monitor the pairs. Go over the answers with the class, then guide students to complete the rule. Draw students' attention to the exceptions mentioned in the tip on page 46.

Answer key

The double room is **bigger** and **more comfortable** than a single room, but of course, it's **more expensive**.
I can give you one of our **most expensive** rooms at a special price.
It's one of our **biggest** rooms.

Rule

Comparative: Add *-er* to a short adjective.
We use the word *more* with a long adjective.
Superlative: Add *-est* to a short adjective.
We use the word *most* with a long adjective.

2B Draw students' attention to the sentences with *than* and guide them to complete the rule.

Rule

We use the word *than* when we compare people or things.

2C Students work in pairs to write sentences, then compare their sentences with another pair. Monitor the pairs. Go over the answers with the class.

Answer key

3 Akio is taller than Naoko.
4 Akio is fitter than Naoko.
5 Naoko is a better student than Akio.
6 Naoko is more polite than Akio.
7 Akio is a worse driver than Naoko.

2D This is a demanding task, so you should check comprehension of the chart and the instructions before you begin. Students should work in groups of three. See TIP 3 on pages xii–xiii for guidelines on group work.

Answer key

2 False. The population of Indonesia is the biggest. / The population of Singapore is the smallest.
3 True
4 False. The population of Singapore is older than the population of Indonesia. / The population of Indonesia is younger than the population of Singapore.
5 False. An apartment in Bangkok is more expensive than an apartment in Jakarta. / An apartment in Jakarta is cheaper than an apartment in Bangkok.
6 False. The most expensive apartment is in Singapore.
7 False. The population of Thailand is the oldest. / The population of Indonesia is the youngest.
8 True

2E Students work individually or in pairs and compare their answers with a partner or another pair, or give this task as homework. Go over the answers with the class.

Answer key

2 Rents aren't as high in Jakarta as in Bangkok.
3 The average age in Thailand is not as low as in Indonesia.
4 The population of Singapore is not as large as the population of Thailand.
5 The number of people per square kilometer is not as high in Thailand as in Singapore.
6 Thailand is not as big as Indonesia.

3 Listing and speaking
Giving advice

page 48

3A Before playing the recording, ask students if any of them have ever been on a long-haul (explain!) flight. Was it exciting/boring/interesting? What was good and bad about it?

You may want to pre-teach the key words at the bottom of page 48 as they will help students to understand the recording.

Follow Steps 2 to 7 of TIP 1 on page xi, with students working in pairs. After Step 5, you can ask students if they have any more dos and don'ts they can add to Sinittra's list.

Answer key

1	Don't	5	Don't
2	Do	6	Don't
3	Do	7	Don't
4	Don't	8	Do

3B Here students have the opportunity to talk about their vacations. Before they begin their preparation, check comprehension of the vocabulary in the chart. For guidelines on *Talking about . . .* activities see TIP 3 on page xii–xiii. Your task is to monitor and prompt students at each step of the activity, and to give correction feedback at the end.

4 Vocabulary focus
Focus 1: Traveling

page 49

4A Students work individually, then compare their answers with a partner. Go over the answers with the class.

Answer key

1	backpacking	4	language course
2	beach vacation	5	skiing
3	camping	6	coach trip

4B This task practices word collocations. Students work in pairs to match the verbs and phrases, then compare their answers with another pair. Monitor the pairs. Go over the answers with the class.

Answer key

1	F	6	B
2	H	7	D
3	E	8	G
4	A	9	J
5	C	10	I

4C Divide the class into two teams. Write *Team 1* and *Team 2* on the board. Deal with the questions one by one. For each sentence, give the team that gets the correct answer first one point.

Answer key

1 A one-way ticket is for one journey. With a round-trip ticket you can travel there and back.
2 It takes off.
3 fare
4 schedule
5 on the platform
6 boarding pass
7 carry-on bag

4 Vocabulary focus
Focus 2: Describing pictures

page 50

4D Look with your students at the phrases we can use when we describe pictures. Put students in pairs and ask Student A not to look at the pictures on this page, but to go straight to Partner file 6 on page 94. When you are certain that students have understood the instructions, start the activity. See TIP 3 on pages xii–xiii for further guidelines on pair work.

Answer key

Student A describes picture B.
Student B describes picture C.

4E The *Key words* task tests the vocabulary that is at the bottom of pages 45–48. This can be done as homework.

Answer key

1 reservation . . . double room
2 confirm
3 average . . . population
4 advice
5 expensive
6 long-haul . . . nervous
7 crowded
8 A: enjoy
  B: comfortable

5 Reading
The Richmond Hotel, Jakarta

page 51

5A Ask students what facilities a business traveler needs in a hotel. Ask them what "other" facilities might mean (restaurant, gym, conference rooms, etc.).

You may want to pre-teach some vocabulary, e.g., *review, location, disadvantage, rooftop, to recommend, lobby, delicious, good value for the money.*

Have students skim the article individually to see which facilities are mentioned. Look at the guidelines on reading in TIP 2 on page xii. Skimming usually involves reading quickly, so set a time limit. Go over the answers with the class.

Answer key

Internet, satellite TV, swimming pool, laundry service, other (restaurant, gym, conference rooms)

5B Ask students to read the article again, this time more slowly, and do the task. Students can compare their answers in pairs or groups. Go over the answers with the class.

Answer key

1	A, C, D	4	B, C
2	A, C	5	B, C
3	B, D	6	A, B

5C Ask students to guess how many stars the writers of the comments gave the hotels and to give the reasons for their choice. This can be done individually, in pairs or groups, with class feedback after the task.

Possible answers

A **** The writer was disappointed with the Wi-Fi signal, but liked the location and the restaurant.
B ***** The writer only says positive things about the hotel.
C * The writer doesn't recommend the hotel. One star for the good location.
D *** The writer says it is not the best hotel he/she knows, but it is good value for the money.

6 Business writing
A confirmation

page 52

6A Before you begin this task, play the first conversation from 1A (track 31) again to remind students of Lucy Chen and Jenny Bond's conversation. Then ask students to work individually or in pairs to choose the best words and phrases to complete the confirmation email. Go over the answers with the class.

Answer key

1	Ms. Bond	4	have any questions
2	would like	5	We hope you enjoy
3	as follows	6	Sincerely

Discuss the wrong answers with your students. It is important for them to know why they are wrong.

1 *Jenny:* first names are too informal for a business email
2 *like:* If we like something, we like it in general. Cf. *I like coffee* with *I would like a cup of coffee (now).*
3 *like this:* too informal for a business email
4 *want anything:* too direct and not polite enough for a business email
5 *Please enjoy:* sounds like an order and is not suitable for a business email
6 *Best:* an informal ending for an email to a friend

Draw students' attention to the punctuation tip on page 52. They will need this for the task in 6B.

6B Play the recording three or four times so that students can make adequate notes. You can put the questions below on the board to guide them. When you are satisfied that students have all the information they need, begin the writing task or assign it as homework. In any case, it should be handed in for individual correction. In the next lesson, you can deal with any general problems and give remedial work to the class or individuals.

Why is Ms. Sari calling the hotel? (to change a reservation)
What kind of room has she reserved? (a single room)
What are the dates of her reservation? (July 1 to 4)
How many nights? (three nights)
How does she want to change her reservation? (She wants to stay longer.)
How many extra nights? (three)

What sort of room does the reservations clerk offer? (a double room)
What is the price? ($900)
For how many nights? (six)
Why will the reservations clerk write to Ms. Sari? (to confirm the reservation)

Possible answer

From: BusinessHotel@Richmond.com
To: emma.sari@msn.com
Subject: Confirmation of your reservation

Dear Ms. Sari:

I would like to confirm your new reservation in the Richmond Hotel as follows:

Room: double room
Number of nights: 6
Date: July 1–7
Total price: $900

If you have any questions, please contact us.

We hope you enjoy your stay with us at the Richmond Hotel.

Sincerely,
your name
Reservations Clerk
Richmond Hotel

TOEIC® practice (pages 53–54)

1 Listening

You will need to pause the recording between each task to give students time to think about and mark their answers.

1A Photographs

In this part of the test, students see a photograph and hear four statements (A–D) about the photograph. Students must choose the statement that best describes the photograph. In the test, the statements are not printed in the test book and are spoken only once, so students need to listen carefully.

For teaching and practice tips for this part of the test, see the notes to Unit 2 *TOEIC® practice* 1A on page 12, and have students look again at the phrases for describing pictures on page 50 in the Student's Book.

Answer key

1 B   2 D

1B Talks

In this part of the test, students hear a talk given by a single speaker. There are three questions and four possible answers (A–D) for each. The students have to choose the correct answer.

In the test, the talk is not printed in the test book and is spoken only once, so students need to listen carefully.

In the real test, students have eight seconds to answer each question. You might want to proceed more slowly in the practice phase.

Encourage students to scan the questions before the recording begins in order to see what kind of information they have to listen for.

Answer key

1 C   2 B   3 D

2 Speaking

Respond to questions

In this part of the test, students hear three questions. For each question, students must begin responding *immediately* after the question. No preparation time is provided, so students must react quickly.

In the real test, students will have 15 seconds to respond to each of the first two questions, and 30 seconds to respond to the third question. That means more information is expected in the answer to the third question.

In the first practice phase, students can think about and write down their answers. Then they can practice saying the responses using their written prompts within the given time (15 or 30 seconds). In the next practice phase, students should say their responses without the written prompts, but they can take as much time as they need. The aim is a final practice phase in which students give their responses within the exam times.

Possible answers

Question 1: What are the hours of the stores here? *Most of the stores are open between nine AM and eight PM. Some supermarkets are open later.*

Question 2: What are the best places to visit on foot? *There's a very interesting museum and a beautiful cathedral not far away.*

Question 3: Are there any good restaurants nearby? *There's a very good Chinese restaurant opposite the hotel, and there's an Italian restaurant nearby. When you leave the hotel, go straight for about 100 meters and it's on the right.*

3 Reading

Reading comprehension

In this part of the test, students read one or more texts such as a magazine or newspaper article, a letter, or an advertisement. The text is followed by several questions. Each question has four answer choices (A–D). The students must select the best answer for each question.

The same practice strategies apply here as in the section *Incomplete sentences* in Unit 2 *TOEIC*® *practice* 3 on page 13.

Answer key

1 A	2 D	3 B	4 C

4 Writing

Write a sentence based on a picture

In this part of the test, students are expected to show their mastery of grammar and vocabulary in a written sentence. Students write one sentence based on a picture. With the picture are two words or phrases that students must use. The forms of the words can be changed, and they can be used in any order.

Possible answers

1 The customer always pays with her / by credit card at the supermarket.
2 The woman is sending a text message from the airport / receiving a text message at the airport.

Tell me about your company

Unit aims

In Unit 7 students will
- listen and understand somebody talking about his own company.
- learn and use regular and irregular verbs in the simple past.
- exchange information about things they did in the past.
- understand people talking about successful Asian companies.
- talk about successful companies.
- learn and use the vocabulary for countries, nationalities, and languages.
- practice collocations with *make* and *do*.
- understand and discuss an article about women in senior management.
- find out about conversation taboos in different parts of the world.

The main focus of this unit is on the vocabulary needed to describe companies and the verb structures required to talk about the past. Students' knowledge of the present simple should facilitate the learning of the past simple, as the use of a form of *do* in negatives and questions is not new.

As in all previous units, there is ample opportunity in this unit for communicative activities. Inevitably, for you as the teacher, the question of accuracy or fluency arises. This question to some extent will be answered by the students themselves. Some students are happy if they can communicate adequately and are not very worried about their mistakes; others worry about making mistakes and are often reluctant to speak at all. So how do you help the former to reduce the number of errors made and encourage the latter to worry less about error avoidance? For a start, you can make it clear that accuracy during the *Grammar focus* and *Vocabulary focus* is important because students need to learn the correct forms, spellings, etc. However, in communicative activities they have the opportunity to experiment more freely and creatively.

During communicative activities, you should intervene as little as possible – generally only if communication breaks down completely. Make notes during the activity and give feedback after the activity is over – but remember that the mistakes have not prevented students' successful completion of the task, therefore many of the errors may not be worth dealing with.

1 Business situation
The story of a company

page 55

1A Before playing the recording, ask students which fashion designers they know and where they come from.

Examples: Jimmy Choo from Malaysia, Yves Saint Laurent from France, Wolfgang Joop from Germany, Giorgio Armani from Italy, Hanae Mori from Japan, etc.

Tell students they will hear an interview with Lee-kyung Kim, a Korean fashion designer. You may want to pre-teach the key words at the bottom of page 55 as they will help students understand the recording. Follow Steps 2 to 5 of TIP 1 on page xi.

Answer key

1 Busan
4 Paris
5 Seoul
6 Sydney

1B Play the recording again. Follow Steps 2 to 7 of TIP 1 on page xi with students working in pairs, although you might prefer not to let students see the script until they have completed 2A.

Answer key

1 False. He was born in 1985.
2 True
3 False. He went to France in 2007.
4 True
5 True
6 False. He worked for a film company.
7 False. It was a great job.
8 True

2 Grammar focus
Focus 1: Past simple – regular verbs
page 56

Although students have encountered the use of *do/does* in the present simple (Unit 1), some of them will still have problems with *did* in questions and *didn't* in negatives, which may lead to forms such as *He no wanted to work there* or *When he went to France?*

2A Make sure students understand the instructions. Play the recording again. Students work individually, then compare their answers with a partner. Go over the answers with the class.

> **Answer key**
>
> 1 returned
> 2 worked
> 3 designed
> 4 didn't want
> 5 did . . . decide
> 6 didn't expect

2B Using the statements and questions in 2A, guide students to complete the rule.

> **Rule**
>
> We use the past simple to talk about **things that happened in the past**.
>
> For regular verbs we add *-d* or *-ed* to the verb.
> We use *did* in questions and *didn't* in negatives.

Draw students' attention to the tip on page 56 about negatives and question forms.

Focus student's attention on the different pronunciations of *-ed*

worked /wɜːk**t**/
designed /dɪˈzaɪn**d**/
decided /dɪˈsaɪd**ɪd**/

But don't spend too much time on this or give too much explanation at this stage as students may feel overtaxed. You can come back to the topic later and practice with students using other verbs from the unit:

/**t**/ *looked, talked, walked, watched*
/**d**/ *listened, moved, opened, played, returned, saved, stayed, studied, welcomed*
/**ɪd**/ *expected, visited, wanted*

2C Students work in pairs, then compare their answers with another pair. Go over the answers with the class. See TIP 3 on pages xii–xiii for guidelines on pair work.

> **Answer key**
>
> 3 A: Did he talk to colleagues?
>   B: No, he didn't talk to colleagues.
> 4 A: Did he open his mail?
>   B: No, he didn't open his mail.
> 5 A: Did he play tennis?
>   B: Yes, he played tennis.
> 6 A: Did he watch a DVD?
>   B: Yes, he watched a DVD.
> 7 A: Did he welcome a client?
>   B: No, he didn't welcome a client.
> 8 A: Did he visit friends?
>   B: Yes, he visited friends.
> 9 A: Did he listen to music?
>   B: Yes, he listened to music.
> 10 A: Did he look at new designs?
>   B: No, he didn't look at new designs.

2D Students work in pairs and ask each other about last Sunday, using questions from 2C. Monitor the pairs. You may also wish to introduce students to the short answers here.

Put on the board:
Yes, I/he/she/it/we/you/they **did**.
No, I/he/she/it/we/you/they **didn't**.

Students should work in pairs and ask the questions in 2C again, this time using the short answers *Yes, he did* or *No, he didn't* in their replies. They can also use the short answers *Yes, I did* or *No, I didn't* in 2D.

2 Grammar focus
Focus 2: Past simple – irregular verbs
page 57

2E Students work in pairs, referring to the list of irregular verbs on page 95 to help them. Monitor the pairs. Go over the answers with the class. There are a lot of irregular verbs to learn, so you could give some to learn as homework and have short tests on them at the beginning of some lessons.

> **Answer key**
>
> 1 left . . . went
> 2 got . . . was . . . didn't have
> 3 did . . . leave
> 4 won

Draw students' attention to the tip on page 57 concerning the past tense of *to be*. You may also like to introduce the short answers.

Put on the board:
Yes, I/he/she/it was.
No, I/he/she/it wasn't.

Yes, we/you/they were.
No, we/you/they weren't.

Practice by asking students questions about themselves and each other, e.g.,

Were you at school / on the beach / in the shopping mall yesterday?

Was Huang / Lin at school / on the beach / in the shopping mall yesterday?

Were Ly and Lin at school / on the beach / in the shopping mall yesterday? etc.

2F Students work in pairs to complete the chart, then compare their answers with another pair. Monitor the pairs. Go over the answers with the class.

Answer key

Last Monday, Lee-kyung . . .	Last Tuesday, Lee-kyung . . .
2 met clients.	2 didn't meet clients.
3 made drawings.	3 didn't make drawings.
4 had lunch with his assistant.	4 didn't have lunch with his assistant.
5 wrote emails.	5 didn't write emails.

2G See TIP 3 on pages xii–xiii for guidelines on pair work. Make sure students work with several different partners.

3 Listening and speaking
Successful Asian companies
page 58

3A Tell students they are going to hear people talking about successful Asian companies. Before playing the recording, ask students if they know or can guess the missing information, e.g., products, headquarters, number of employees. You may want to pre-teach the key words at the bottom of page 58 as they will help students to understand the recording.

Stress that students do not need to understand every word, and they should write down only key words to complete the chart. Follow Steps 2 to 5 of TIP 1 on page xi.

3B Play the recording again. Follow Steps 2 to 6 of TIP 1 on page xi.

Answer key

1 product
2 headquarters
3 fourth largest
4 the United States
5 customers
6 countries
7 Four friends
8 leading

3C Here students have the opportunity to research and talk about a successful company – either a real one or an invented one. You will need to allow students time to do some research – perhaps assign the task for homework. Students can pool their ideas in the next lesson.

For guidelines on *Talking about* . . . activities, see TIP 3 on pages xii–xiii. Your task is to monitor and prompt students at each step of the activity, and to give correction feedback at the end.

4 Vocabulary focus
Focus 1: Countries and nationalities
page 59

4A Students work in pairs to find the correct matches, then compare their answers with another pair. Monitor the pairs. Go over the answers with the class.

Answer key

2 H	5 I	8 D
3 E	6 J	9 G
4 B	7 C	10 A

4B Before you start, draw students' attention to the tip on page 59 about nationalities and languages. Students work in pairs to complete

Answer key

Company	Lenovo	Hyundai	Olam	Asian Paints
Product	*computer hardware*	automobiles	food	paint
Started	1984 in Beijing, China	*1967 in Seoul, South Korea*	1989 in West Africa	1942 in Bombay, India
Headquarters in . . .	(North Carolina) the United States	(Seoul) South Korea	*Singapore*	Bombay (Mumbai), India
Employees	27,000	75,000	18,000	*5,000*
Active in . . . countries	160	193	65	17
Revenue (US$)	30 billion	76 billion	14 billion	*1.9 billion*

the sentences, then compare their answers with another pair. Monitor the pairs. Go over the answers with the class.

Game: Ask students to look at the map on page 6 (Unit 1). Students work in groups and have 15 minutes to write down the countries and languages. The group that has the most countries and languages correct wins.

4C Put students in two or more teams. Make sure students understand the instructions. So that they cannot read ahead, ask them to close their books or cover up the exercise. You or one student should read the questions, e.g., *Can you name an American coffee house?* The team that shouts out a correct answer first gets a point. The team with the most points wins.

4 Vocabulary focus
Focus 2: *Make* and *do*

page 60

4D Using the sample sentences, guide students to complete the rule.

Rule

We usually use *do* as a general verb or for an activity.

We use *make* when there is a product at the end.

4E Students work individually or in pairs and compare their answers with a partner or another pair. Go over the answers with the class.

4F Remind students of the tip on page 3: "*What do you do?* asks about a person's job.*"

Students work in pairs to ask and answer questions about the people in 4E. Monitor the pairs. Go over the answers with the class.

The *Key words* task tests the vocabulary that is at the bottom of pages 55–58. This can be done as homework.

Answer key

1 studied . . . fashion designer
2 success
3 experience
4 specializes
5 win
6 headquarters
7 revenue
8 employees

5 Reading
Top jobs for women

page 61

5A Read the instructions with your students and make sure they understand what they have to do. Students work in pairs to exchange their ideas on what the article might be about. Monitor the pairs. Have students skim the article and tell you if they found any of their ideas. Remind students that skimming should be done quickly – see TIP 2 on page xii – and set a time limit.

5B You may wish to pre-teach some of the vocabulary, e.g., *senior management*, *average*, *ambitious*.

Students work individually, then compare their answers with a partner. Go over the answers with the class.

Background information
The G7 – or Group of Seven – is a group consisting of the finance ministers of the seven wealthiest developed nations in the world.

BRIC – or Big Four – is an acronym that refers to Brazil, Russia, India, and China – countries that are considered to be at a similar level of economic development.

Answer key

Asia Pacific 29%, ASEAN 36%, G7 21%, BRIC 28%

5C As students have now read the article twice individually, they can work in pairs to find the correct answers, then compare their answers with another pair. Monitor the pairs. Go over the answers with the class.

Answer key

1 C 3 B
2 A 4 C

5D Encourage students to speculate, e.g., *Perhaps Asian women are more intelligent / work harder / are more ambitious / have more opportunities / have better child care than women in other countries.*

6 Culture focus
Conversation taboos

page 62

6A Have students read the taboos aloud. Correct pronunciation and check comprehension. Put the first taboo, *talk about money with strangers*, on the board. Elicit the other taboos in a short form and put them on the board. Ask students if these are also taboo in their country.

ask about a person's family
ask somebody's age
show when they are angry
say bad things about the government

Tell students they will hear five businesspeople talking about their trips to other countries and the things they did wrong. Tell students that you will play the whole recording through once, and they should listen to find out where the five people are from. Play the whole recording.

Answer key

Sylvia Astengo – Italy
Michael Gomez – Manila, the Philippines
Ryan Forbes – Los Angeles, the US
Sandra Miles – the UK
Adi Kurniawan – Indonesia

6B Play the recording again. Follow Steps 2 to 5 of TIP 1 on page xi.

Answer key

1 B 4 A
2 D 5 C
3 E

6C Play the recording again, stopping after each speaker to deal with the case individually. Ask students to use the information from 6A to explain what each person did wrong.

Answer key

1 What Sylvia Astengo did was wrong because in Asian countries you should try to stay calm. Only children lose control.

2 What Michael Gomez did was wrong because in most Western countries it is not polite to ask somebody's age – especially a woman.

3 What Ryan Forbes did was wrong because people in the UK don't like to talk about money. What you earn in your job is private.

4 What Sandra Miles did was wrong because in many countries it is a taboo to say bad things about the government.

5 What Adi Kurniawan did was wrong because in Saudi Arabia it is a taboo to ask about a wife or daughter.

Finally, you can have students read the script aloud. Correct pronunciation and intonation on the spot.

Let's eat out

Unit aims

In Unit 8 students will
- listen to and understand an invitation to lunch and a conversation in a restaurant.
- learn how to use the modal verbs *can*, *must*, *have to*, and *need to*.
- learn about and use countable and uncountable nouns.
- understand a conversation in a food court.
- explain and recommend dishes on a food court menu.
- talk about food, drinks, and favorite dishes.
- make, accept, or decline spoken and written invitations.
- read and understand a text about a private jet service.
- practice listening, reading, and writing for the TOEIC® test.

This unit focuses on the vocabulary surrounding the topic of eating out in business situations, and on making, accepting, and declining spoken and written invitations. The main grammar topics are modal verbs, countable and uncountable nouns, and the articles and determiners that can be used with them.

As in all previous units, there is ample opportunity in this unit for students to practice listening comprehension. This is one of the most difficult skills to master in a foreign language. Students often suffer from the mistaken belief that they have to understand everything, or they will understand nothing, so an unknown word or unfamiliar phrase makes them panic and blocks their progress.

The listening tasks in **Business Plus** are designed to guide students from global listening for the gist to listening for detail. "Seven-step listening" in TIP 1 on page xi helps you to provide adequate support in the various phases of listening activities. Setting the scene before listening is important, and students should always look at the task before they listen so they know what they are listening for. After listening, students should always check their answers in pairs or groups before the feedback phase. That way, no student can feel individually responsible for wrong answers! Encourage and motivate your students by being prepared to play the recording as often as they wish.

 1 **Business situation**
Entertaining in the business world
| page 63 |

1A Before playing the recording, talk about the picture. Ask: *Who are the people? Where are they? What are they doing? What are they eating? What can you see in the background?*

You may want to pre-teach the key words at the bottom of page 63 as they will help students understand the recording. Follow Steps 2 to 5 of TIP 1 on page xi.

Answer key

1	A	6	A
2	M	7	R
3	A	8	R
4	M	9	M
5	A	10	M

1B Play conversation 1 again. Students can write down their answers and compare with a partner. Go over the answer with the class.

Answer key

They will meet at twelve-thirty on Wednesday at Amy's office.

1C Play conversation 3 again. Students can write down their answers and compare with a partner. Go over the answers with the class.

Answer key

1 pasta with salmon, mineral water
2 chicken risotto with salad, mineral water

Finally, follow Steps 6 and 7 of TIP 1 on page xi with students working in pairs, although you might prefer not to let students see the script until they have completed 2A.

Grammar focus
Focus 1: Modal verbs

`page 64`

2A Play the recording again. Students work individually, then compare their answers with a partner. Go over the answers with the class.

When listening, students may have trouble distinguishing between *can* and *can't* because sometimes the final *-t* gets lost. Draw their attention to the very slight difference between *You can turn here* and *You can't turn here*.

Answer key

Conversation 1
Marc: We **must** meet for lunch.

Conversation 2
Man: You **don't need to** reserve a table.
Man: You **have to** make a reservation if you want to come in the evening.

Conversation 3
Marc: I don't speak it, but I **can** understand quite a lot.
Marc: I **mustn't** be late.

2B Students work in pairs to talk about the road signs. Monitor the pairs. Go over the answers with the class.

Answer key

When you see this sign, you . . .
1 **must** stop.
2 **have to** turn right.
3 **mustn't** park.
4 **don't need to** park (but you can if you want to).
5 **can** go left or right.
6 **can't** turn.

2C Students work individually or in pairs and compare their answers with a partner or another pair. Go over the answers with the class.

Answer key

Dear Sandra,

I called Marc Simpson about meeting for lunch. He **can't** come tomorrow, but he **can** come on Wednesday. You and I **have to** talk before I see him. It's important. But you **don't need to** come to my office. We **can** talk on the phone. **Can** you call me sometime today?

I **mustn't** forget to tell Simon about Marc's visit, but I **can't** do it today because he isn't in the office.

Amy

2D In larger classes, this task can be done in groups rather than as a class. Monitor the groups. After the task is completed, call on some students to report on a few members of their group, e.g., *Kasem can swim, but he can't drive. Ly has to go to the dentist today, but she doesn't need to go shopping.*

 Grammar focus
Focus 2: Countable and uncountable nouns

`page 65`

2E You may wish to introduce some of the vocabulary using pictures of the food mentioned on this page.

Focus students' attention on the concepts of countable and uncountable nouns. Show them how we count *one apple*, *two apples*, *three apples*, etc., but we don't count **one bread*, **two breads*, **three breads*. Students also need to understand that some nouns can be countable or uncountable depending on the context, e.g., *Green tea is good for you* and *Two green teas, please* (= cups of green tea).

Guide students to complete the rule.

Rule

We can count some words, for example **apples** and **bananas**. (or *carrots, eggs, melons, sandwiches*)

We can't count some words, for example **pasta** and **water**. (or *bread, fish, fruit, meat, tea*)

2F Using the two sentences, guide students to complete the rule.

Rule

The verb after an uncountable noun is in the **singular**.

2G Students work in pairs to find the correct answers, then compare their answers with another pair. Go over the answers with the class.

Answer key

3	an	7	X
4	X	8	a
5	a	9	an
6	X	10	X

Explain that we can't use *a* or *an* with the X words, but we can use *the* and *some*. Remind students that *some* refers to an unknown quantity, while the other words (*a kilo*, *two liters*, *three cups*) refer to specific quantities. You may want to look at the rules of *some* and *any* again on page 28.

2H Draw students' attention to the tip on page 65, which deals with quantities plus *of*.

Students work in pairs to find the correct answers, then compare their answers with another pair. Go over the answers with the class.

> **Answer key**
>
> 1 Can I have **some** bread, please?
> 2 Cook the **pasta** for ten minutes.
> 3 I would like one kilo of **meat**.
> 4 Correct
> 5 Use a liter **of** water to cook the rice.
> 6 Do you want some **butter** on your bread?

2I Make sure students understand all the words. You can point to the picture of a bottle and a glass on page 65, there is a bowl on page 67, there is probably a box somewhere in the classroom, and you can draw a cup on the board. Students work in pairs to find the correct answers, then compare their answers with another pair. Tell students that sometimes there can be more than one answer. Go over the answers with the class.

> **Possible answers**
>
> a bowl of rice
> a cup of coffee
> a piece of meat
> a box of eggs
> a glass of wine

3 Listening and speaking
In a food court

page 66

3A Before playing the recording, ask students what they know about food courts. Ask: *Do you sometimes eat in a food court? Where? What is your favorite dish?*

You may want to pre-teach the key words at the bottom of page 66 as they will help students to understand the recording. Follow Steps 2 to 5 of TIP 1 on page xi.

> **Answer key**
>
> | | | |
> |---|---|---|
> | A | What do you recommend? | 3 |
> | B | We can have something sweet for dessert. | 7 |
> | C | That sounds good. | 6 |
> | D | Can you explain it to me? | 5 |
> | E | Food courts are really popular here in Bangkok. | *1* |
> | F | What's that over there? | 8 |
> | G | What would you like to eat? | 2 |
> | H | That's a bit too spicy for me. | 4 |

Draw students' attention to the tip at the bottom of page 66 about the spelling of *dessert*.

3B Follow Steps 1 to 7 of TIP 1 on page xi, with students working in pairs.

> **Answer key**
>
> chicken   coconut   egg   mango   noodles
> peanuts   pork   rice   seafood   shrimp   tofu

3C Students work in pairs to have a conversation guided by the conversation map. See TIP 3 on pages xii–xiii for guidelines on pair work. Your task is to monitor the pairs, note their mistakes and give feedback at the end of the activity.

4 Vocabulary focus

Focus 1: Food and drink

page 67

4A Students work in pairs to correct the wrong names, then compare their answers with another pair. Go over the answers with the class. Then students work in groups. On a piece of paper one student in the group writes the four headings *Fruit*, *Vegetables*, *Drinks*, *Fast food*. The group decides which food comes under which heading. Feedback can be on the board; then ask students for other words they know to add to each list.

> **Answer key**
>
> | | | | |
> |---|---|---|---|
> | 2 | pizza | 7 | beans |
> | 3 | mushrooms | 8 | mineral water |
> | 4 | strawberry | 9 | hamburger |
> | 5 | onions | 10 | grapes |
> | 6 | fruit juice | | |
>
> **Fruit:** watermelon, grapes, strawberry
> **Vegetables:** mushrooms, onions, beans
> **Drinks:** fruit juice, mineral water
> **Fast food:** pizza, hamburger

4B Students work individually or in pairs and compare their answers with a partner or another pair. Go over the answers with the class.

Answer key

2 onion
3 shrimp
4 pineapple
5 mushroom
6 juice

4C Students work individually or in pairs and compare their answers with a partner or another pair. Go over the answers with the class.

Answer key

2 **beer** – It's a drink. The others are meat.
3 **chicken** – It's meat. The others are fruit.
4 **cabbage** – It's a vegetable. The others are desserts.
5 **pork** – It's meat. The others are fish.
6 **lemon** – It's a fruit. The others are drinks.

4D Here students have the opportunity to talk about their favorite dish. Step 1 could be assigned as homework. For guidelines on *Talking about* . . . activities, see TIP 3 on pages xii–xiii. Your task is to monitor and prompt the pairs, and to give correction feedback at the end.

4 Vocabulary focus
Focus 2: Invitations

page 68

4E Have students read the conversation and answer questions 1–3. Go over the answers with the class.

Answer key

1 I'd like to invite you to lunch.
2 What about tomorrow?
3 A Thanks for the invitation.
  B I'm afraid I can't come tomorrow.
  C Wednesday is better for me. I can come on Wednesday.

4F Students work in pairs and compare their answers with another pair. Go over the answers with the class. Point out that informal phrases are usually much shorter than formal phrases.

Answer key

Formal invitation

1 If you have no plans for this evening, Mr. Simpson, I'd like to invite you to have dinner with us.
2 That's very kind of you. I'd like that very much.
3 Good. Shall l pick you up at your hotel at about eight?
4 Eight is fine. I'm looking forward to it.

Informal invitation

1 I don't know what your plans are, Amy, but would you like to join us for a drink later on?
2 I'd love to. What time?
3 Let's say seven-thirty in the hotel bar.
4 Great. I'll be there at seven-thirty.

4G Students work in pairs. See TIP 3 on pages xii–xiii for guidelines on pair work.

4H The *Key words* task tests the vocabulary that is at the bottom of pages 63–66. This can be done as homework.

Answer key

1 diet
2 recommend
3 delicious
4 dishes . . . menu
5 road sign
6 suit
7 spicy
8 invitation

5 Reading
Special requests on MJets

page 69

5A Before students read, have them look at the picture of a private jet on page 69. Ask, *What kind of people fly in private jets?* Write students' ideas on the board, then ask them to read the article quickly to see if any of the ideas are in it. Ask for feedback.

5B Look at the guidelines on reading in TIP 2 on page xii. You may want to pre-teach some vocabulary, but be careful not to clash with the *Vocabulary in context* task in 5D.

5C Students do the task individually, then compare their answers with a partner. Go over the answers with the class.

5D Students work individually or in pairs and compare their answers with a partner or another pair. Go over the answers with the class.

6 Business writing
Invitations

page 70

6A Students work in pairs to complete the emails, then compare their answers with another pair. Go over the answers with the class. These emails will serve as models for the tasks in 6B and 6C.

6B Students work in pairs to write an invitation. Monitor the pairs. Students can hand in their email for correction or, if you prefer to have peer correction, go on to task 6C.

6C Students work in the same pairs as in 6B. They swap the invitation they wrote in 6B with another pair. The pair who receives the invitation should first correct any mistakes they can find, then decide whether to accept or decline the invitation. They should write a reply using Robert Schmidt's acceptance email or Christine Adams' rejection email as a model. Your task is to monitor the pairs and help students correct the invitation emails. The replies to the invitation can be handed in for correction.

1 Listening

You will need to pause the recording between each task to give students time to think about and mark their answers.

1A Question-Response

In this part of the test, students hear a question and three possible responses (A–C). Students must choose the best response to the question. In the test, the questions are not printed in the test book and will be spoken only once, so students need to listen carefully.

As many of the questions in this section begin with a question word, it is important that students can distinguish *who, what, when, where, why, how,* etc. As you can see in the example, confusing *when* and *where* could lead to a wrong answer choice.

A useful practice strategy is to isolate the questions, e.g., *Excuse me. Is there a supermarket near here?* Ask students who and where the speaker might be. Ask them to predict a possible correct response without looking at the distracters. Then do the listening task.

Answer key			
1 B	2 A	3 B	4 C

1B Conversations

In this part of the test, students hear some short conversations between two people. Students see and hear three questions on each conversation. There are four possible answers (A–D). Students have to choose the correct answer.

For tips and practice strategies, see Unit 4 *TOEIC®* *practice* 1B on page 24.

Answer key	
Conversation 1	**Conversation 2**
1 C	1 C
2 D	2 D
3 B	3 B

2 Reading

Text completion

In this part of the test, students see a text (e.g., an email, article, advertisement, notice) in which words and phrases are missing in some of the sentences. Four answer choices (A–D) are given below the sentences. Students have to select the best answer to complete the text.

The same practice strategies apply here as in the section *Incomplete sentences* in Unit 2 *TOEIC®* *practice* 3 on page 13.

Answer key			
1 D	2 A	3 B	4 C

3 Writing

Respond to a written request

In this part of the test, students show how well they can write a reply to an email. The reply will be scored on the quality and variety of the grammatical structures and the vocabulary, as well as on the organization of the email and the correct use of email conventions.

For further details, see Unit 4 *TOEIC®* *practice* 4 on page 24.

Possible answer
Dear Max,
Let me tell you something about Nanking Fashions. It is a Chinese company. The headquarters are in Shanghai. It started ten years ago. It's a big company. It has 800 employees. I think your company is a very big company. When did it start? How many employees does it have? Are the headquarters in Helsinki or in another town? Please tell me more about it.
Best wishes, Suzie

Work and play

Unit aims

In Unit 9 students will
- listen and talk about activities at work and during leisure time.
- learn and use -ing or to-infinitive after certain verbs.
- learn and practice the connecting words because, but, if, so, and than.
- understand an interview about travel and leisure in Asia.
- exchange information about theme parks in Asia.
- use play, go, or do with leisure-time activities.
- understand a text about tourism in Thailand.
- write about what to do and see in their country.
- understand and talk about body language in Asia.

This unit focuses on activities during and after work. Students have the opportunity to read about, listen to, and discuss different aspects of the leisure industry and talk about their own leisure-time activities. The main grammar focus is on gerunds and infinitives after certain verbs. The main vocabulary focus is on describing different activities.

All the topics of the *Reading* section of the Student's Book are chosen with student motivation in mind. Students will be more likely to want to read a text if it looks interesting and if they can relate to the topic. In this unit the *Asian Business Online* article looks at tourism in Thailand.

It is essential that students know that they should not read every text in the same way and at the same speed. As mentioned in TIP 2 on page xii (*Teaching reading comprehension*) students must know why they are reading (for the gist? for a particular piece of information? for details?), and how they should read (skim, scan, or read intensively).

Business Plus offers a variety of reading activities. In this unit, for example, a *Before you read* task focuses students' minds on the topic; after reading, students look for the main idea and answer a number of comprehension questions. The reading tasks are followed by a speaking or writing task on a similar topic.

1 Business situation
During and after work

page 73

1A Before playing the recording, ask students to describe what they can see in the pictures. Refer them to page 50 for the vocabulary to describe pictures.

Follow Steps 2 to 5 of TIP 1 on page xi. You may want to pre-teach the key words at the bottom of page 73 as they will help students understand the recording.

You can follow up with Steps 6 to 7 of TIP 1 on page xi, or wait until after you have listened to the conversation in 1B.

Answer key

1 Ly
2 Ly
3 Amsyar
4 Amsyar
5 Ly
6 Amsyar
7 Ly
8 Ly

1B Follow Steps 2 to 5 of TIP 1 on page xi. After Step 5, you can follow Steps 6 and 7 with students working in pairs.

Answer key

1 to spend
2 to play
3 to do
4 to stay
5 to watch
6 to write
7 to finish
8 to see

Grammar focus
Focus 1: *-ing* or *to*-infinitive

[page 74]

2A Students can either refer back to page 73 or look at the script on pages 108 and 109.

Rule

After the verbs *dislike*, *enjoy*, *hate*, *like*, and *mind*, we use the **-ing** form of the verb.

After the verbs *hope*, *learn*, *prefer*, *promise*, *try*, and *want*, we use the **to-infinitive** form of the verb.

Note: In this unit *like* + *-ing* is used, but students will sometimes hear *like* + *to*-infinitive. There is a small difference in meaning. *Like* + *-ing* means *I enjoy* (e.g., *I enjoy reading*). *Like* + *to*-infinitive means *I prefer* (e.g., *I like to keep my room tidy*).

Draw students' attention to the tip on page 74. We use *like* + *-ing* when we talk about things in general, e.g., *I like working in my office* and *He likes traveling*. We use *would like to do* to talk about a certain time, e.g., *I'd like to work in an office* (one day) and *He'd like to travel to the US next year*.

2B Students work individually or in pairs and compare their answers with a partner or another pair. Go over the answers with the class.

Answer key

3 to work
4 working
5 to learn
6 traveling
7 to spend
8 helping
9 to be

2C Students work in pairs to ask and answer questions. See TIP 3 on pages xii–xiii for guidelines on pair work.

 Grammar focus
Focus 2: Connecting words

[page 75]

2D Have students read the sentences silently or aloud. Play the recordings again. Students listen and check, then compare their answers with a partner. Go over the answers with the class.

Answer key

because   so   if

Draw students' attention to the tip on page 75 about the use of commas.

2E Students work in pairs and compare their answers with another pair. Go over the answers with the class.

Answer key

1 because
2 so
3 but
4 than
5 if
6 and

2F Students work in pairs or individually to write the sentences, then compare their answers with a partner or another pair. Go over the answers with the class.

Answer key

2 I wrote the report because my boss asked me to do it.
3 The report is finished, but my boss doesn't like it.
4 My boss didn't like the report, so I had to write it again.
5 It was a longer report than the one I wrote last week.
6 I can write a report if you want me to.

2G Students do the task individually, then talk about their answers in a small group. In smaller classes, students can be asked to report about each other to the class; in larger classes to their group.

Lee is learning English because she . . .
Kim is learning English, but . . .
etc.
Monitor the groups and give feedback at the end of the activity.

3 **Listening and speaking**
Travel and leisure in Asia

[page 76]

3A Before playing the recording, ask students to look at all the pictures on this page. Ask: *What parts of the leisure industry can you see in the pictures?* (health spa, theme parks) *Do you know any other parts of the leisure industry?* (golf and other sports, travel and tourism, bars and restaurants, movie theaters, etc.)

You may want to pre-teach the key words at the bottom of page 76 as they will help students to understand the recording. Follow Steps 2 to 5 of TIP 1 on page xi.

Answer key

1 C   2 A   3 B

3B Follow Steps 2 to 7 of TIP 1 on page xi. Students work in pairs. In Step 7 they should read the conversation at least twice, swapping roles, as Ms. Majid has a lot to say and the interviewer has only a little.

Answer key

1 Kuala Lumpur
2 plans and develops
3 their health
4 much cheaper
5 games and entertainment
6 travel and leisure

3C Put students in pairs and ask Student A not to look at the information on this page, but to go straight to Partner file 7 on page 94. When you are certain that students have understood the instructions, start the activity. See TIP 3 on pages xii–xiii for further guidelines on pair work.

4 **Vocabulary focus**
Focus 1: *play/do/go ...*

page 77

4A Before playing the recording, check that students know all the vocabulary in the box. Follow Steps 1 to 5 in TIP 1 on page xi.

Using the mind map, guide students to complete the rule.

Rule

We often use *go* with activities that end in *-ing*.
We often use *play* with games.
We use *do* with many other sports.

4B Students work in pairs. See TIP 3 on pages xii–xiii for guidelines on pair (and group) work.

At the end of the activity, ask students in small classes to report about each other to the class; in large classes to their group. Put one example on the board as a model.

Lien doesn't play the guitar, but she does aerobics.

4 **Vocabulary focus**
Focus 2: Describing leisure activities

page 78

4C Students work in pairs or small groups to complete the chart. After they have compared their answers with another pair or group, go over the answers with the class.

Answer key

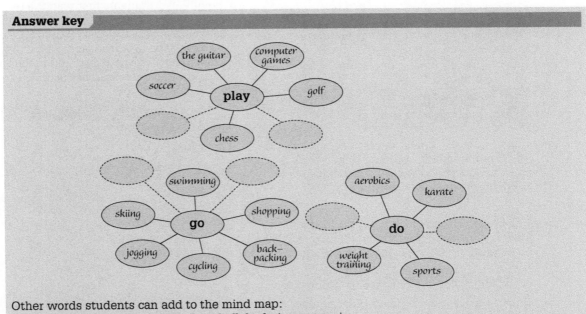

Other words students can add to the mind map:
play: the piano, an instrument, baseball, badminton, tennis
do: judo, gymnastics, yoga
go: sailing, dancing, skiing, horseback riding, fishing

positive	negative
exciting	dangerous
fun	difficult
great	hectic
interesting	boring
	(too) expensive

4D Students work in pairs. First, students name the activities. Go over the answers with the class. Then students ask and answer questions about likes and dislikes, using words from 4C. Monitor the pairs. Follow the activity with a feedback phase, where you deal with the main errors.

Answer key

1 skateboarding
2 boxing
3 dancing
4 playing tennis
5 traveling
6 playing computer games
7 having a barbecue
8 listening to music

4E The *Key words* task tests the vocabulary that is at the bottom of pages 73–76. This can be done as homework.

Answer key

1 presentations	5 entertainment
2 boring	6 health
3 take part . . . activities	7 travel agency
4 foreign	8 fantastic

 ## 5 Reading
Tourists in Thailand

`page 79`

5A Before reading, students should work in small groups to answer the questions. Follow the activity with a feedback phase.

5B Students read individually for the main idea. Look at the guidelines on reading in TIP 2 on page xii. Go over the answers with the class.

Answer key

In **2013** a quarter of a million Chinese tourists visited Thailand. **Some of them** came as a result of the movie *Lost in Thailand*. Flying to Thailand is **cheaper** than in the past. Tourists to Thailand **don't need** to get a visa before they leave home.

5C Students work individually or in pairs and compare their answers with a partner or another pair. Go over the answers with the class.

Answer key

1 It is about two Chinese businessmen who go to Thailand to find their boss.
2 More and more airlines are offering low-cost flights to Bangkok.
3 Thailand offers tourists visas when they arrive.
4 Because *Lost in Thailand* shows this beautiful place at its best.

5D This task gives students an opportunity to write about their own country. It can be done in class or assigned as homework. In any case, it should be handed in for individual correction. In the next lesson, you can deal with any general problems and give remedial work to the class or individuals.

6 Culture focus
Body language in Asia

`page 80`

6A Clarify with students what is meant by "body language." Make sure students understand the main headings (*eye contact*, *gestures*, *distance*, *touching*, *shaking hands*). You can demonstrate the meanings.

6B and 6C Students first read the text silently, then take turns to read parts of it aloud. Clarify any unfamiliar vocabulary. Students then work in pairs to do the tasks. After they have compared their answers with another pair, go over the answers with the class.

Answer key

6B
1 Korea
2 India
3 China
4 Malaysia
5 Malaysia

6C
1 Laos, Thailand
2 Thailand
3 Korea
4 Korea
5 Taiwan

6D Students work in pairs. Monitor the pairs. Follow the activity with a feedback phase, where you deal with the main errors.

Come again soon!

Unit aims

In Unit 10 students will
- listen and understand people saying goodbye.
- learn and use the *will*-future.
- test their grammar with a Grammar quiz.
- listen to an interview about the future of the workplace.
- exchange ideas about their own future.
- learn and practice phrases for saying hello and goodbye.
- test their vocabulary with a Vocabulary quiz.
- read and understand a text about ASEAN.
- discuss what ASEAN means to them personally.
- understand and write a thank-you email.
- practice listening, speaking, reading, and writing for the TOEIC® test.

The main focus of this unit is on the future. The *will*-future is introduced and students listen to and talk about topics relating to life in the future, both in the workplace and in their personal lives. Students will read and discuss what the ASEAN Economic Community means to different people and to the students themselves.

This unit includes a *Grammar quiz* and a *Vocabulary quiz*, which test and review some key structures and vocabulary from the Student's Book. These quizzes not only test students' progress, they also provide an opportunity for individualized remedial work.

As you are approaching the end of **Business Plus 1**, it is time to talk to your students about their future as learners of English, and to prepare them for more independent learning. By now students will have realized that language learning involves more than just being taught in the classroom. Ask students about their language-learning activities outside the classroom and how they plan to continue learning English. Discuss the activities they can do to improve their language skills, e.g., watching English movies in the original with subtitles, writing emails to an English-speaking pen pal, reading online magazines in English, playing English language-learning games online, and downloading the lyrics of their favorite English songs and memorizing them.

Students can also look at useful EFL-learning sites such as
http://www.bbc.co.uk/worldservice/learningenglish/
and
http://learnenglish.britishcouncil.org/en/

---

1 Business situation
Saying goodbye

page 81

 1A Before playing the recording, remind students of Tony Marshall's trip to Bangkok in Unit 6 (page 48), where he met and had lunch with Chermarn Arak (Unit 8, page 66). Tell students that they are going to hear a conversation between Tony and Chermarn just before he leaves Bangkok.

Follow Steps 2 to 5 of TIP 1 on page xi.
You may want to pre-teach the key words at the bottom of page 81 as they will help students understand the recording.

Answer key

1 evening
2 a quarter to seven
3 a taxi
4 no problem
5 her help
6 a book
7 in touch

1B Follow Steps 2 to 7 of TIP 1 on page xi with students working in pairs, although you might prefer not to let students see the script until they have completed 2A.

2 Grammar focus
Focus 1: The *will*-future

page 82

2A Play the recording up to "I'll read and play computer games." Students complete the sentences and then compare their answers with a partner. Go over the answers with the class.

2B Using the examples in 2A, guide students to complete the rule. Draw attention to the pronunciation of *I'll* /aɪl/.

Rule

We use *will* to talk about the future.
The short form is *'ll*.   The negative is **won't**.

2C Give students time to read about Cindy. Check comprehension. Students work in pairs to do tasks 1 and 2. See TIP 3 on pages xii–xiii for guidelines on pair work. Give students the opportunity to work with several different partners.

Draw students' attention to the tip about short answers on page 82.

2 Grammar focus
Focus 2: Grammar quiz

page 83

2D Students work individually. Give them adequate time to answer all the questions and have a task ready for students who finish quickly. For example, they can look for the grammar sections where the structures were introduced in the Student's Book and write down the grammar topic and the page numbers, using the plan of the book on pages iv–vii to help them. This will be useful for reference in the feedback phase.

When all students have completed the task, go over the answers with the class. If this is to be a real test of what they have learned, students should not compare their answers first. After correction, ask students to read the grammar pages relevant to their mistakes.

3 Listening and speaking
The workplace in 2025

page 84

3A Before playing the recording, tell students that they will hear an interview with Chen Ming, who has written a book about the workplace of the future. Ask students what they think will be different at work in the future.

You may want to pre-teach the key words at the bottom of page 84 as they will help students to understand the recording.

Follow Steps 2 to 7 of TIP 1 on page xi.

3B For Step 1 play the recording. Students work individually or in pairs and compare their answers with a partner or another pair. Go over the answers with the class. You can do the task in two parts, first Sanda Myint and then Saiful Muhamat.

Answer key

1 definitely
2 probably
3 definitely
4 probably
5 definitely
6 definitely
7 probably
8 definitely
9 probably

In Step 2 students work individually and make notes. In Step 3 students work in pairs to tell each other about their future. See TIP 3 on pages xii–xiii for guidelines on pair work.

 4 | **Vocabulary focus**
Focus 1: Saying hello and goodbye
page 85

4A Students work in pairs to put the phrases into the correct column, then compare their answers with another pair. Go over the answers with the class.

Answer key

Saying hello	Saying goodbye
How do you do?	I hope to see you again soon.
How was the weather in Sydney?	I'll be in touch.
How was the trip?	It was a pleasure.
Nice to meet you.	Please give them my regards.
This is my colleague, Robert.	Thanks for everything.

4B Follow the same procedure as in 4A.

Answer key

2 F
3 A
4 B
5 C
6 D

4C Play the recording again. Students fill in the missing prepositions. Go over the answers with the class.

Answer key

1 to
2 to . . . about
3 at
4 on
5 on
6 on

4D Students work in pairs to find the correct answers, then compare their answers with another pair. Monitor the pairs. Go over the answers with the class.

Answer key

2 It depends **on** the weather.
3 I'd like to welcome you **to** our company.
4 I spent all my money **on** new software.
5 Now I'm working **on** my presentation. / I'm working **on** my presentation now.
6 What do you want to talk **about** today?

4E The *Key words* task tests the vocabulary that is at the bottom of pages 81–84. This can be done as homework.

Answer key

1 regards
2 24/7
3 project
4 pleasure
5 in touch
6 remote
7 touch screen
8 trends

 4 | **Vocabulary focus**
Focus 2: Vocabulary quiz
page 86

4F Students work individually. Give them adequate time to answer all the questions and have a small task ready for students who finish quickly. For example, have students see how many key words beginning with the letter *c* they can find in the book.

When all students have completed the task, go over the answers with the class. If this is to be a real test of what they have learned, students should not compare their answers first.

5 Reading
The ASEAN Economic Community

page 87

5A Ask students what "ASEAN" stands for and write *Association of Southeast Asian Nations* on the board. Students work in pairs or small groups. They have ten minutes to discuss and write down their answers. They can compare their answers with another pair or group. Go over the answers with the class.

5B Look at the guidelines on reading in TIP 2 on page xii. Have students read topics 1 to 3 individually, then skim the article and match a topic to each of the three people. Skimming usually involves reading quickly, so set a time limit. Go over the answers with the class.

5C Students work individually, then compare their answers with a partner. You may want to pre-teach some of the vocabulary: *conditions, salary, skilled, valuable, border, fast-track, major, job opportunities, official language*.

When the task is completed, go over the answers with the class.

5D If students do not have their own ideas about ASEAN, ask them about the ideas in the article and whether they could be important for them in future. Students could give them a ranking from one (= very important for me) to four (not important for me).

- Things will be cheaper.
- People will be able to work where they want.
- Travel will be easier.
- There will be better job opportunities.

6 Business writing
A thank-you email

page 88

6A Students work in pairs to find the phrases, then compare their answers with another pair. Go over the answers with the class.

6B This writing exercise can be assigned as homework or done in class. In any case, it should be handed in for individual correction. In the next lesson, you can deal with any general problems and give remedial work to the class or individuals.

6C Students work in pairs, then compare their answers with another pair. Go over the answers with the class.

Answer key

1 received
2 attached
3 send
4 to confirm
5 meeting

TOEIC® practice (pages 89–90)

1 Listening

You will need to pause the recording between each task to give students time to think about and mark their answers.

1A Photographs

In this part of the test, students see a photograph and hear four statements (A–D) about the photograph. Students must choose the statement that best describes the photograph. In the test, the statements are not printed in the test book and are spoken only once, so students need to listen carefully.

For teaching and practice tips for this part of the test, see the notes to Unit 2 *TOEIC® practice* 1A on page 12, and have students look again at the phrases for describing pictures on page 50 in the Student's Book.

Answer key

1 B   2 D

1B Talks

In this part of the test, students hear a talk given by a single speaker. There are three questions and four possible answers (A–D) for each. Students have to choose the correct answer to the question. In the test, the talk is not printed in the test book and is spoken only once, so students need to listen carefully.

Encourage students to scan the questions before the recording begins in order to see what kind of information they have to listen for.

In the real test, students have eight seconds to answer each question. You might want to proceed more slowly in the practice phase.

Answer key

1 D   2 C   3 B

2 Speaking

2A Describe a picture

In this part of the test, the student describes a picture in as much detail as possible. In the real test the student will have 30 seconds to prepare and 45 seconds to speak about the picture. For practice purposes this time can be extended. See also the tips and strategies suggested in Unit 2 *TOEIC® practice* 1A and 2A on page 12 of this Teacher's Manual, and have students look again at words and phrases for describing pictures on page 50 in the Student's Book.

Possible answer to photograph 1

I can see a young woman. She is slim, has dark hair, and is wearing a green T-shirt. She is in the supermarket. There are shelves on the left, on the right, and in the background with a lot of different packages and bottles in different colors. She is trying to read the label on the product. The woman looks serious. Perhaps she is worried about something. I think she is on a diet and wants to know how many calories there are in the product.

2B Read a text aloud

In this part of the test, student's pronunciation and intonation is tested. Students are given a text to read aloud. In the real test, students have 45 seconds to prepare and 45 seconds to read the text aloud. For practice purposes this time can be extended.

A useful practice strategy is to work together with your students to underline the words that a native speaker would normally stress, and to mark the place where a small pause (//) would be natural. Advise students to try not to read too fast.

A new report on the future of travel // shows that there will be a <u>big</u> increase in "do-it-yourself" travel – // that means that travelers will <u>organize</u> their trips themselves. // They will use social <u>media</u> sites, // forums, and online <u>communities</u> // in the way that travelers in the <u>past</u> used a <u>travel</u> agent. Travel agencies will <u>not</u> disappear, // but the way they <u>communicate</u> with their customers // will change. For example, // they will allow <u>mobile</u> transactions // or transactions through social <u>media</u> sites.

3 Reading

Incomplete sentences

In this part of the test, students see sentences with a missing word or phrase. Four answer choices (A–D) are given below each sentence. Students must choose the best answer to complete the sentence.

When practicing, give students time to complete the task, go over the answers with the class, then discuss wrong answers with them. It is important for them to know not only that an answer is wrong but also why it is wrong.

For further tips see Unit 2 *TOEIC® practice* 3 on page 13 of this Teacher's Manual.

Answer key

1 C	3 D	5 A
2 A	4 B	6 C

4 Writing

Write a sentence based on a picture

In this part of the test, students are expected to show their mastery of grammar and vocabulary in a written sentence. Students write one sentence based on a picture. With the picture are two words or phrases that the student must use. The forms of the words can be changed, and they can be used in any order.

Possible answer

1 The subway is always very crowded in the mornings.
2 New technologies will be very important in the workplace of the future.